Dictionary of Capital Market

Also from New Century

- Dictionary of Economics
- Dictionary of Public Finance
- Dictionary of Money, Banking and Finance
- Dictionary of Marketing and Advertising
- Dictionary of Insurance
- Dictionary of International Trade and Business
- Encyclopaedia of Economics and Commerce (*in two volumes*)

Dictionary of
Capital Market

By

Deepak R. Raste

Associate Professor,
Shree Sahjanand Vanijya Mahavidyalay,
Ahmedabad, Gujarat

New Century Publications
New Delhi, India

NEW CENTURY PUBLICATIONS
4800/24, Bharat Ram Road,
Ansari Road, Daryaganj,
New Delhi - 110 002 (India)

Tel.: 011-2324 7798, 4358 7398, 6539 6605
Fax: 011-4101 7798
E-mail: indiatax@vsnl.com • info@newcenturypublications.com
www.newcenturypublications.com

Editorial office:
LG–7, Aakarshan Bhawan,
4754-57/23, Ansari Road, Daryaganj,
New Delhi – 110 002

Tel.: 011-4356 0919

First Published: **July 2014**

ISBN: 978-81-7708-385-9

Published by New Century Publications and printed at Salasar Imaging Systems, New Delhi.

Designs: Patch Creative Unit, New Delhi.

PRINTED IN INDIA

About the Dictionary

An efficient capital market is an important constituent of a sound financial system. Capital market channelises household savings to the corporate sector and allocates funds to firms. In this process, it allows both firms and households to share risks associated with business. Moreover, capital market enables the valuation of firms on an almost continuous basis and plays an important role in the governance of the corporate sector.

Dynamics of capital market require changes in the laws, rules and regulations on a continuing basis. Consequently, new terms and concepts and their definitions are added to capital market lexicon on a regular basis.

This dictionary is designed to provide a useful, reliable, readable and *single source* guide to the all-important field of capital market. It provides simple and easily comprehensible definitions and explanations of terms used in this area. The terms, concepts and usages are given their most common definition. Readers will also find helpful illustrations of important terms.

This reference work is intended as a practical tool for a cross-section of readership. It will be useful for teachers and students of economics, commerce, law, and management, and also for bankers, corporate executives, legislators and government officials. Meticulously cross-referenced, the dictionary is a comprehensive and invaluable source of essential information.

About the Author

Deepak R. Raste is Associate Professor in Accountancy and Commerce at Shree Sahjanand Vanijya Mahavidyalay, Ahmedabad, Gujarat. He did his M. Com. and Ph.D. from Gujarat University, Ahmedabad. He has published papers in refereed journals of repute including a co-authored paper in *International Journal of Business Research* published by International Academy of Business and Economics, USA.

Dr. Raste is also a Ph.D. guide with Gujarat University, Ahmedabad. He has participated in 4 international level and 6 national level conferences/seminars and presented research papers.

Contents

How Best to Use this Dictionary

An efficient capital market is an important constituent of a sound financial system. Capital market channelises household savings to the corporate sector and allocates funds to firms. In this process, it allows both firms and households to share risks associated with business. Moreover, capital market enables the valuation of firms on an almost continuous basis and plays an important role in the governance of the corporate sector.

Dynamics of the capital market require changes in the laws, rules and regulations on a continuing basis. Consequently, new terms and concepts and their definitions are added to capital market lexicon on a regular basis.

This dictionary is designed to provide a useful, reliable, readable and *single source* guide to the all-important field of capital market. It provides simple and easily comprehensible definitions and explanations of terms used in this area. The terms, concepts and usages are given their most common definition. Readers will also find helpful illustrations of important terms.

This reference work is intended as a practical tool for a cross-section of readership. It will be useful for teachers and students of economics, commerce, law, and management, and also for bankers, corporate executives, legislators and government officials. Meticulously cross-referenced, the dictionary is a comprehensive and invaluable source of essential information.

The entries in the dictionary are arranged in strict alphabetical order, letter by letter. A complete list of entries is given on pages xvii to xxxvi of the dictionary. All entries are followed by the page number at which they respectively appear.

To make the best use of the material included in the dictionary and also to avoid repetition, entries are elaborately and meticulously cross-referenced in the following manner.

1. Cross-references immediately following an entry either indicate interchangeable terms—e.g. **Unit of Trading** See Marketable Lot—or direct the reader to the relevant description where that particular term is treated as part of a

larger (essay type) entry, e.g. **Call Options:** See Options.

2. Cross-references at the end of an entry point to the treatment of a related subject explained elsewhere in the dictionary, e.g. **Bombay Stock Exchange (BSE):...**See also National Stock Exchange of India Limited (NSE).
3. Terms which appear during description of another term and are followed by (q.v.*) are entered separately at relevant places in the dictionary, e.g. **London Inter-bank Offer Rate (LIBOR):** Often used as a basis for pricing Euroloans...There are similar rates like...Mumbai Inter-bank Bid and Offer Rates (MIBOR) (q.v.).
4. A term with popular abbreviation/acronym is entered in expanded form as, for example, **Unit Trust of India (UTI).** However, abbreviation/acronym of a term also appears as a separate entry, though the reader is directed to the expanded form of the entry as, for example, **UTI:** See Unit Trust of India. Also, an abbreviation/acronym is entered in expanded form on its first appearance in each entry. A list of abbreviations/acronyms related to capital market is given on pages xi to xvi of the dictionary.
5. The dictionary also contains some essay type entries pertaining to important terms/institutions. These are meant to provide the reader an integrated view of the entry concerned as, for example, **Securities and Exchange Board of India (SEBI)** which is the apex regulatory and supervisory authority for capital market in India.

Though adequate care has been taken to include in the dictionary as many terms and concepts as possible, a few omissions are likely in this kind of endeavour. The author will feel obliged to be informed of such omissions that could find place in the next edition. Similarly, suggestions are welcome to improve the completeness and accuracy of the terms explained in the dictionary.

Several sources, such as books, articles, websites, have been referred to compile this work. I would like to thank all the published and other sources from which definitions have been gathered. Thanks are also due to the members of the research team of New Century Publications who actively contributed with their expertise during the preparation of the dictionary.

Ahmedabad
June 10, 2014

Deepak R. Raste

---

*q.v. = quod vide (Latin) = which may be referred to

Abbreviations/Acronyms Related to Capital Market

ACH	Automated Clearing House
ACU	Asian Clearing Union
ADRs	American Depository Receipts
ADs	Authorised Dealers
AIDBs	All India Development Banks
AIFIs	All India Financial Institutions
ALM	Asset Liability Management
AMC	Asset Management Company
AML	Anti-Money Laundering
AMS	Aggregate Measure of Support
ATMs	Automated Teller Machines
BCBS	Basel Committee for Banking Supervision
BCSBI	Banking Codes and Standards Board of India
BFRS	Board for Financial Regulation and Supervision
BFS	Board for Financial Supervision
BIFR	Board for Industrial and Financial Reconstruction
BIS	Bank for International Settlements
BOISL	Bank of India Shareholding Ltd.
BPSS	Board for Regulation and Supervision of Payment and Settlement Systems
BSE	Bombay Stock Exchange
CAAP	Capital Adequacy Assessment Process
CAC	Capital Account Convertibility
CAMELS	Capital Adequacy, Asset Quality, Management, Earnings, Liquidity and Systems Control
CAPM	Capital Asset Pricing Model
CAR	Capital to Assets Ratio
CBLO	Collateralised Borrowing and Lending Obligations
CCFF	Compensatory and Contingency Financing Facility
CCIL	Clearing Corporation of India Ltd.
CDBMS	Centralised Data Base Management System
CDOs	Collateralised Debt Obligations
CDR	Corporate Debt Restructuring; Credit-Deposit

	Ratio
CDs	Certificates of Deposit
CFMS	Centralised Funds Management System
CFSs	Consolidated Financial Statements
CIBIL	Credit Information Bureau of India Ltd.
CIS	Collective Investment Scheme
CLN	Credit Linked Note
CMO	Collateralised Mortgage Obligation
CP	Commercial Paper
CPSS	Committee on Payment and Settlement Systems
CPSUs	Central Public Sector Undertakings
CR	Contingency Reserve
CRAR	Capital to Risk-Weighted Assets Ratio
CRISIL	Credit Rating Information Services of India Ltd.
CRR	Cash Reserve Ratio
Demat	Dematerialisation
DFIs	Development Finance Institutions
DIC	Deposit Insurance Corporation
DICGC	Deposit Insurance and Credit Guarantee Corporation
DP	Depository Participant
DR	Depository Receipt
DRI	Differential Rate of Interest
DRT	Debt Recovery Tribunals
DSR	Debt Service Ratio
DSS	Debt Swap Scheme
E-banking	Electronic Banking
ECBs	External Commercial Borrowings
E-commerce	Electronic Commerce
ECR	Export Credit Refinance
ECS	Electronic Clearing Service
EFF	Extended Fund Facility
EFT	Electronic Funds Transfer
EMEs	Emerging Market Economies
E-money	Electronic Money
EMU	European Monetary Union

ESPS	Employee Stock Purchase Scheme
ETFs	Exchange Traded Funds
EXIM Bank	Export Import Bank of India
FCA	Foreign Currency Assets
FCCBs	Foreign Currency Convertible Bonds
FCNR(A)	Foreign Currency Non-Resident (Accounts)
FCNR(B)	Foreign Currency Non-Resident Accounts (Banks)
FDI	Foreign Direct Investment
FEMA	Foreign Exchange Management Act
FERA	Foreign Exchange Regulation Act
FIIA	Foreign Investment Implementation Authority
FIIs	Foreign Institutional Investors
FIPB	Foreign Investment Promotion Board
FIPC	Foreign Investment Promotion Council
FMC	Forward Markets Commission
FVCI	Foreign Venture Capital Investor
GDR	Global Depository Receipt
GIC	General Insurance Corporation of India
HDFC	Housing Development Finance Corporation
HFCs	Housing Finance Companies
HFT	Held for Trading
HTM	Held Till Maturity
IBA	Indian Banks' Association
IBEF	India Brand Equity Foundation
IC	Investment Commission
ICAAP	Internal Capital Adequacy Assessment Process
ICAI	Institute for Chartered Accountants of India
ICDs	Inter-Corporate Deposits
ICICI	Industrial Credit and Investment Corporation of India
ICRA	Information and Credit Rating Agency
IDBI	Industrial Development Bank of India
IDBs	India Development Bonds
IDFC	Infrastructure Development Finance Company
IFCI	Industrial Finance Corporation of India
IMF	International Monetary Fund

IPF	Investor Protection Fund
IPO	Initial Public Offering
IRDA	Insurance Regulatory and Development Authority
IRR	Internal Rate of Return
IRS	Interest Rate Swaps
ISDA	International Swap and Derivatives Association
ISIN	International Securities Identification Number
IT	Information Technology
ITES	Information Technology Enabled Services
JLG	Joint Liability Group
JV	Joint Venture
KYC	Know Your Customer
LAF	Liquidity Adjustment Facility
LAN	Local Area Network
LERMS	Liberalised Exchange Rate Management System
LIBOR	London Inter-Bank Offered Rate
LLP	Limited Liability Partnership
MAT	Minimum Alternative Tax
MFs	Mutual Funds
MIBOR	Mumbai Inter-bank Bid and Offer Rates
MNCs	Multinational Companies
MoU	Memorandum of Understanding
NABARD	National Bank for Agriculture and Rural Development
NAV	Net Asset Value
NBFCs	Non-banking Financial Companies
NBFIs	Non-banking Financial Institutions
NDS	Negotiated Dealing System
NEAT	National Exchange for Automated Trading
NEFT	National Electronic Funds Transfer
NHB	National Housing Bank
NLR	Net Liquidity Ratio
NPAs	Non-performing Assets
NRI	Non-resident Indian
NSCCL	National Securities Clearing Corporation Ltd.
NSDL	National Securities Depository Ltd.

NSE	National Stock Exchange of India Ltd.
NSSF	National Small Savings Fund
NYSE	New York Stock Exchange
OMO	Open Market Operations
OTC	Over the Counter
PAC	Persons Acting in Concert
PFRDA	Pension Fund Regulatory and Development Authority
PIO	Person of Indian Origin
PLR	Prime Lending Rate
PSBs	Public Sector Banks
PSU	Public Sector Undertaking
RBI	Reserve Bank of India
RBIA	Risk-based Internal Audit
RBS	Risk-based Supervision
REPO	Repurchase Agreement
RIBs	Resurgent India Bonds
RRBs	Regional Rural Banks
RTGS	Real Time Gross Settlement
SBI	State Bank of India
SCBs	Scheduled Commercial Banks
SEBI	Securities and Exchange Board of India
SENSEX	Sensitive Index
SEZ	Special Economic Zone
SHG	Self-help Group
SIDBI	Small Industries Development Bank of India
SLR	Statutory Liquidity Ratio
SPV	Special Purpose Vehicle
SRFAESI	Securitisation and Reconstruction of Financial Assets and Enforcement of Security Interest Act
SRP	Supervisory Review Process
SSIs	Small Scale Industries
STCI	Securities and Trading Corporation of India
STP	Straight through Processing
TBs	Treasury Bills
TRS	Total Return Swap

TSMG	Tata Strategic Management Group
UCBs	Urban Co-operative Banks
UTI	Unit Trust of India
VaR	Value at Risk
VAT	Value Added Tax
WMA	Ways and Means Advances
YTM	Yield-to-maturity

List of Entries

K

L

M

The Dictionary
A-Z

Aa

Accelerated Depreciation: It is a method under which entrepreneurs are allowed—during the first year or the first few years after acquiring business assets—to have depreciation allowances on a basis which exceeds the actual depreciation. This system provides incentive for capital investment by reducing the tax payable in the early years of the life of the assets concerned.

Access Control: It is a mechanism to control the access to the system and its facilities by a given user up to the extent necessary to perform his job function. It provides for the protection of the system resources against unauthorized access. Unauthorized access causes destruction, alterations, theft of data or funds, breach of data confidentiality, denial of service etc. Access control may be of discretionary and mandatory types.

Accreting: A description applicable to a range of instruments, e.g. caps, swaps, collars and swaptions, where the notional amount on which the instrument is based increases successively during its life.

Accretion to Equity: Retained earnings/total equity at the end of previous year x 100.

Accrued Interest: The interest accruing on a security since the previous coupon date. If a security is sold between two payment dates, the buyer usually compensates the seller for the interest accrued, either within the price or as a separate payment.

Acid Test Ratio: The value of cash equivalents and accounts receivable (the quick assets) divided by current liabilities. Also known as quick asset ratio or liquidity ratio, it is a measurement of corporate liquidity.

Acquirer: Any entity (individual, company etc.), which intends to acquire or acquires substantial quantity of shares or voting rights of target company or acquires or agrees to acquire control over the target company along with the persons acting in concert.

Ad hoc Margin: Margin collected by the stock exchange from the members having unduly large outstanding position or the margin levied on volatile scrips based on ad hoc basis keeping in view the risk perspective.

Additional Margin: In case of sudden higher than expected volatility, additional margin may be called for by the stock exchange. This is generally imposed when the exchange fears that the markets have become too volatile and may result in some crisis, like payments crisis etc. This is a pre-emptive move by stock exchange to prevent breakdown.

Admission to Dealing: The process of granting permission to the securities of a company to be listed in a stock exchange and to provide trading facilities for the securities in the market.

Advance/Decline Line: A technical analysis tool representing the total of differences between advances and declines of security prices. The advance/decline line is considered the best indicator of market movement as a whole.

Agency Orders: Orders that a broker dealer executes for the account of a customer with another professional or retail investor.

All-inclusive Concept: The application of this concept is one of the two main approaches to measuring earnings. When earnings are measured on the basis of this concept, income is considered to be the amount remaining after all items (including write-offs and capital gains and losses, and excluding dividends and any other transactions between the enterprise and its shareholders or investors) causing any increase or decrease in the shareholders' or investors' interests during the accounting period, are allowed for.

Allotment Advice: A letter sent to the successful applicant by the company stating allotment of shares or debentures or other securities against his application. The advice is not negotiable in the market.

Allotment Letter: Document of title issued to investors by companies stating allotment of shares/debentures/other securities to applicants subscribing for such securities or in pursuance of certain contracts entered into in that behalf. These letters are negotiable in the market.

American Depository Receipt (ADR): A certificate issued in US in lieu of a foreign security. The original securities are lodged in bank/custodian abroad, and the ADRs are traded in the US for all intents and purposes as if they were a domestic stock. An ADR dividend is paid in US dollars, so it provides a way for American investors to buy foreign securities without having to go abroad, and without having to switch in and out of foreign currencies.

Analyst: A firm/company/an individual who is engaged either on his own behalf or on behalf of any other firm or organization that is regularly publishing securities recommendations based on research either through print media and/or electronic media.

Appreciation: A rise in the price of a security or in the value of one currency in terms of another.

Arbitrage: Technically, arbitrage consists of purchasing a commodity or security in one market for immediate sale in another market (deterministic arbitrage). Popular usage has expanded the meaning of the term to include any activity which attempts to buy a relatively under-priced item and sell a similar, relatively overpriced item, expecting to profit when the prices resume a more appropriate theoretical or historical relationship (statistical arbitrage).

In the context of international short-term capital flows, it refers to profiting by buying some financial asset/currency at a lower price and selling at a higher price in two different markets when both prices are known to the trader. So, there is no risk involved in it. For example, if dollar is cheaper in Kuwait than in Singapore, arbitrageurs will buy it in Kuwait and sell in Singapore. This will continue till the two rates are equal. If the exchange rates in various centres (more than two) are made mutually consistent, it is called *triangular arbitrage.*

In trading options, convertible securities, and futures, arbitrage techniques can be applied whenever a strategy involves buying and selling packages of related instruments. Risk arbitrage applies the principles of risk offset to mergers and other major corporate developments. The risk offsetting position(s) do not insulate the investor from certain event risks (such as termination of a merger agreement on the risk of completion of a transaction within a certain time) so that the arbitrage is incomplete. Tax arbitrage transactions are undertaken to share the benefit of differential tax rates or circumstances of two or more parties to a transaction.

Regulatory arbitrage transactions are designed to provide indirect access to a risk management market where one party is denied direct access by law or regulation. Swap driven arbitrage transactions are motivated by the comparative advantages which swap counter-parties enjoy in different debt and currency markets.

Arbitrageurs: Arbitrageurs thrive on market imperfections. An arbitrageur profits by trading a given commodity, or other item, that sells for different prices in different markets. This becomes possible by simultaneous purchase of securities in one market where the price is low and sale in another market, where the price is comparatively higher.

This is done when the same securities are being quoted at different prices in the two markets. Arbitrageurs derive advantage from difference in prices of securities prevailing in the two markets.

An arbitrageur is basically risk averse. He enters into those contracts were he can earn riskless profits. When markets are imperfect, buying in one market and simultaneously selling in other market gives riskless profit. Arbitrageurs are always in the look out for such imperfections.

In the futures market one can take advantages of arbitrage opportunities by buying from lower priced market and selling at the higher priced market. In index futures arbitrage is possible between the spot market and the futures market.

Arbitration: An alternative dispute resolution mechanism provided by a stock exchange for resolving disputes between the trading members and their clients in respect of trades done on the exchange.

Asset Allocation: The process of determining the optimal division of an investor's portfolio among different assets. Most frequently this refers to allocations between debt, equity and cash.

Asset Allocation Fund: A mutual fund that splits its investment assets among stocks, bonds, and other vehicles in an attempt to provide a consistent return for the investor.

Asset Backed Securities: Securities backed by assets that are not mortgage loans. Examples include assets backed by automobile loans, credit card receivables and others.

Asset Based Securitization: A process that creates a series of securities which is collaterised by assets mortgaged against loans, assets leased out, trade receivables, or assets sold on hire purchase basis or instalment contracts on personal property.

Asset-Liability Management (ALM): It is concerned with strategic balance sheet management involving all market risks. It also deals with liquidity management, funds management, trading and capital planning.

Asset Management: The function of managing assets on behalf of a customer, usually for a fee.

Asset Management Company: A company which handles the day-to-day operations and investment decisions of a unit trust.

Asset Securitisation: Securitisation is a process through which illiquid assets are transformed into a more liquid form of assets and distributed to a broad range of investors through capital markets. The lending institution's assets are removed from its balance sheet and are instead funded by investors through a negotiable financial instrument. The security is backed by the expected cash flows from the assets. Securitisation as a technique gained popularity in the advanced countries in the 1970s. Favourable tax treatment, legislative enactments, establishment of Government-backed institutions that extend guarantees, and a pragmatic regulatory environment appear to have contributed to the successful development of this market.

Securitisation involves pooling similar assets together in a separate legal entity or special purpose vehicle (SPV) and redirecting the cash flows from the asset pool to the new securities issued by the SPV. The SPV is a device to ensure that the underlying assets are insulated from the risks of default by the originator of the assets. In general, there are two main advantages of securitisation. First, it can turn ordinary illiquid assets into reasonably liquid instruments. Second, it can create instruments of high credit quality out of debt of low credit quality.

Securitisation is gaining acceptance as one of the fastest growing and most innovative forms of asset financing in the global capital market. Asset securitisation can play an important role in promoting integration of the credit market and the debt market in India. Securitisation increases the number of debt instruments in the market. In the case of securitisation, the price of a securitised instrument would tend to converge with the price of a bond.

Securitisation, by creating marketability, generates liquidity in the otherwise illiquid portfolio of loan assets of lenders. It also furthers the growth of the bond market by providing investment avenues to investors suiting their risk-return profiles. It, therefore, complements the bond market.

Advantages of Securitisation: Securitisation is designed to offer a number of advantages to the seller, investor and the debt market. For the seller or originator, securitisation mainly results in receivables being replaced by cash, thereby improving the liquidity position. It removes the assets from the balance sheet of the originator, thus, freeing capital for other uses, and enabling restructuring of the balance sheet by reducing large exposures or sectoral concentration. It facilitates better asset liability management (ALM) by reducing market risks resulting from interest rate mismatches. The process also enables the issuer to recycle assets more frequently and thereby improves earnings. For investors, securitisation essentially provides an avenue for relatively lower risk investment. Credit enhancement provides an opportunity to investors to acquire good quality assets and to diversify their portfolios. From the point of view of the financial system as a whole, securitisation increases the number of debt instruments in the market, and provides additional liquidity in the market. It also facilitates unbundling, better allocation and management of project risks. It widens the market by attracting new players due to availability of superior quality assets.

Pitfalls of Securitisation: Securitisation, however, if not carried out prudently can leave risks with the originating bank without allocating capital to back them. The main risk for a bank arises if a true sale has not been achieved and the selling bank is forced to recognise some or all of the losses if the assets subsequently cease to perform. Also, funding risks and constraints on liquidity may arise if assets designed to be securitised have been originated, but because of disturbances in the market, the securities cannot be placed. There is also a view that there is at least a potential conflict of interest if bank originates, sells, services and underwrites the same issue of securities.

In the Indian context, the securitisation market has witnessed a significant growth in recent years. This, therefore, should help in furthering the development of the bond market. The international experience shows that the credit appraisal and documentation process in the hands of the loan originator can be lax, which in turn can lead to loss of investor confidence in such instruments. Therefore, care would need to be taken to ensure that appropriate credit appraisal and documentation process is followed at the time of origination of loans.

Asset Stripper: A person who buys a company in order to make profit by peeling off its assets bit by bit, and then selling them. These assets may be separate subsidiaries or plant and equipment or property. This process invariably involves the stripping of another sort of asset (the employees) of a number of jobs. This has been largely responsible for giving asset strippers a bad name. The asset stripper relies on the difference in the price of the business as a whole (as valued by a stock market, for example) and the sum of the amounts that can be raised from its parts sold separately. Such a possibility arises most commonly when a company is making losses or a much smaller profit than seems to be justified by its size.

Asymmetric Information: A situation where access to information by one party (or parties) to a transaction is better than access by another party (or parties). Asymmetric information can be used as a source of power in determining the outcome of the transaction.

At Best: An instruction from the client to the broker authorizing him to use his discretion so as to execute an order at the best possible market price.

At-the Money Option (ATM): An ATM option is an option that would lead to zero cash flow if it were exercised immediately. An option on the index is ATM when the current index equals the strike price (i.e. spot price = strike price).

Auction: When a seller is not in a position to deliver the securities he has sold, the buyer sends in his applications for buying-in, so that the securities can be bought from the market and delivered to him. This process by which the securities are procured on behalf of the defaulter is known as auction.

Auditor: A person who is professionally qualified to examine and scrutinize accounts. He/she inspects records and reports on the profitability and financial position of the company.

Authentication: It is a process of verifying claimed identity of an individual user, machine, software component or any other entity. For example, an IP address identifies a computer system on the Internet, much like a phone number identifies a telephone. It may be to ensure that unauthorized users do not enter, or for verifying the sources from where the data are received. It is important because it ensures authorization and accountability. Authorization means control over the activity of user, whereas accountability allows us to trace uniquely the action to a specific user. Authentication can be based on password or network address or on cryptographic techniques.

Authorized Assistants: Assistants or clerks of members who are authorized by them to do business on their behalf in the market. The member has to take responsibility of fulfilling all the transactions and business commitments of the authorized assistants entered into on behalf of the members.

Authorized Bank: A bank, including a co-operative bank, authorized by the Reserve Bank of India to maintain an account of a person resident outside India.

Authorized Capital: The amount of capital that a company has been authorized to raise by way of equity and preference shares, as mentioned in the articles of association/memorandum of association of the company.

Authorized Dealer: A person authorized as an authorized dealer under sub-section (1) of Section 10 of Foreign Exchange Management Act (FEMA), 1999.

Authorized Person: An authorized dealer, money changer, offshore banking unit or any other person for the time being authorized under sub-section (a) of Section 10 of Foreign Exchange Management Act (FEMA), 1999 to deal in foreign exchange or foreign securities.

Automated Clearing House (ACH): A computerized facility used by member depository institutions to electronically combine, sort, and distribute inter-bank credits and debits. ACHs process electronic transfers of government securities and provide customer services, such as direct deposit of customers' salaries and government benefit payments (i.e., social security, welfare, and veterans' entitlements), and preauthorized transfers.

Automated Teller Machine (ATM): A machine, activated by a magnetically encoded card or other medium that can process a variety of banking transactions. These include accepting deposits and loan payments, providing withdrawals, and transferring funds between accounts.

Automated Teller Machine (ATM) Networks: The National Financial Switch (NFS) network started its operations on August 27, 2004 and is owned and operated by Institute for Development and Research in Banking Technology (IDRBT), Hyderabad. NFS is one of the several shared ATM networks which inter-connect the ATM switches of the banks together and thus, enable inter-operability of the ATM cards issued by any bank across the entire network.

The primary objective of any ATM network, like the NFS, is to make the ATM deployment more economical and viable for banks by pooling their respective ATM resources. The main advantage of an ATM network is that it obviates the need for having bank-specific multiple ATM installations in the same geographical area, thereby reducing the entailed costs for the banks but without compromising on the reach of the banks to their customers. From the perspective of customers, the ATM card of any bank can be used in any ATM—which enables more convenient and wider ATM access to the bank customers of varied banks in different geographical areas.

It is noteworthy that the use of the ATMs connected through any of the ATM networks in the country became cost free for the customers from April 1, 2009. Thus, the networking of the ATMs across the country, by leveraging the technology, is indeed a very customer-friendly development.

Automatic Reinvestment: A fund service giving unit holders/ shareholders the option to purchase additional units/shares using dividend and capital gain distributions.

Averaging: The process of gradually buying more and more securities in a declining market (or selling in a rising market) in order to level out the purchase (or sale) price.

Bb

Back Office: The part of a firm that is responsible for post-trade activities. Depending upon the organisational structure of the firm, the back office can be a single department or multiple units (such as documentation, risk management, accounting or settlements). Some firms have combined a portion of these responsibilities, usually found in the back office, particularly those related to risk management, into what they term as a middle office function.

Backwardation: The payment of money charges made by a seller of shares which he borrows to deliver against his sale. These charges become payable only when there are more sellers who are not in a position to deliver against their sale. These charges become payable to the buyer, when the seller is not in a position to deliver the documents to the buyers who demand delivery.

Badla: Carrying forward of transactions from one settlement period to another without effective delivery. This is permitted only in specified securities and is done at the making up price which is usually the closing price of the last day of settlement.

Badla Charge: Consideration or interest paid to the seller by the buyer for carrying over a transaction from one settlement period to another.

Badliwalas: A financier who lends money to both buyers and sellers of shares when they are not able to pay or deliver.

Balance of Payments: A statistical system through which economic transactions occurring during specific time periods between an economy and the rest of the world can be summarised in a systematic way. The fifth edition of the IMF *Balance of Payments Manual (BPM5)* provides conceptual guidelines for compiling balance of payments statistics according to international standards.

Balance Sheet: An accounting statement of a company's assets and liabilities, provided for the benefit of shareholders and regulators. It gives a snapshot, at a specific point of time, of the assets that the company holds and how the assets have been financed.

Balanced Fund: A fund which aims to provide both growth and regular income. Such a fund invests both in equities and fixed income securities in the proportion indicated in its offer document.

Bancassurance: The phenomenon whereby a financial institution combines the selling of banking products and insurance products through the same distribution channel. Bancassurance rests on the premise that it is easy to cross-sell banking and insurance services because customers feel confident buying insurance from the same institution where they keep their savings.

Banker to an Issue: A scheduled bank carrying on all or any of the issue-related activities, namely acceptance of application and application monies, acceptance of allotment or call monies, refund of application monies, and payment of dividend or interest warrants.

Bank of India Shareholding Ltd (BOISL): The settlements of trade in the equities market (both cash and derivative segments) are settled in the BSE by clearing house called BOISL which is a company jointly promoted by BSE (49 percent) and Bank of India (51 percent). BOISL, *inter alia*, handles some of the settlement-related activities of BSE as per instructions and directions of BSE. Responsibility of the clearing house is to handle such settlement activities including co-ordination with the market participants, viz. depositories, clearing banks etc.

However, the overall responsibility of settlement and risk management functions, viz. collection of margins, collateral management etc. pertaining to transactions done on BSE Online Trading (BOLT) System lies with the BSE. See also National Securities Clearing Corporation Ltd. (NSCCL).

Bankrupt: A bankrupt person, firm, or company has insufficient assets to cover its debts. The debtor seeks relief through a court proceeding to work out a payment schedule or erase debts. In some cases, the debtor must surrender control of all assets to a court-appointed trustee.

Bankruptcy: It means the legal proceedings by which the affairs of a bankrupt person are turned over to a trustee or receiver for administration under the bankruptcy laws. There are two types of bankruptcy: (a) involuntary bankruptcy—one or more creditors of an insolvent debtor file a petition having the debtor declared bankrupt, and (b) voluntary bankruptcy—the debtor files a petition claiming inability to meet financial obligations and willingness to be declared bankrupt.

Basel I Norms: Internationally, there were no explicit capital adequacy standards before the introduction of Basel I norms in 1988. The most common approach was to lay down minimum capital requirements for banks in the respective banking legislations and determine the relative strength of capital position of a bank by ratios such as debt-equity ratio, or its other variants for measuring the level of leverage.

In the autumn of 1974, the Bank of England began to conceptualise the formation of a G-10 group of bank supervisors leading to the formation of the Standing Committee on Banking Regulation and Supervisory Practices, or the Basel Committee, in December 1974. The initial mandate of the Committee was for sharing of and application of each others knowledge, rather than any comprehensive attempt to harmonise cross-country supervision. Nevertheless, it led to an unimaginable degree of regulatory harmonisation later.

In December 1987, International Convergence of Capital Measures and Capital Standards, i.e. Basel Accord (now Basel I) was achieved. In July 1988, the Basel I Capital Accord was created.

The major achievement of the Basel Capital Accord, 1988

was the introduction of discipline through imposition of risk-based capital standards both as measure of the strength of banks and as a trigger device for intervention by supervisors under the scheme of prompt corrective action (PCA).

Over the years, however, several deficiencies of the design of the Basel I framework surfaced. The Basel I capital adequacy norms were criticised for the simple *one-size-fits-all* approach that did not adequately differentiate between assets that have different risk levels. Despite the amendment to the original framework in 1996, the simple risk weighting approach of Basel I did not keep pace with more advanced risk measurement approaches at large banking organisations. By the late 1990s, some large banking organisations, especially in advanced countries, had begun developing economic capital models, which used quantitative methods to estimate the amount of capital required to support various elements of risks of an organization.

The Basel Committee itself recognised the deficiencies in the Basel I framework. The rapid rate of innovation in financial markets and the growing complexity of financial transactions reduced the relevance of Basel I as a risk managing framework, especially for large and complex banking organisations. Various shortcomings also distorted the behaviour of banks and made it much more complicated to monitor them.

Given the financial innovations and growing complexity of financial transactions and also with a view to addressing the shortcomings of Basel I, the Basel Committee on Banking Supervision (BCBS) released the New Capital Adequacy Framework for International Convergence of Capital Measurement and Capital Standards (Basel II) on June 26, 2004 to replace the 1988 Capital Accord by year-end 2007. Basel II norms (q.v.) aim at aligning minimum capital requirements to underlying risk profiles of banks. The framework is also designed to create incentives for better risk measurement and management.

Basel II Norms: While the Basel I framework was confined to the minimum capital requirements for banks, the Basel II accord expands this approach to include two additional areas, *viz.* the supervisory review process and increased disclosure requirements for banks. In terms of Basel II, the stability of the banking system rests on the following three pillars, which are designed to reinforce each other:

Pillar 1: Minimum Capital Requirements—a largely new, risk-adequate calculation of capital requirements which (for the first time) explicitly includes operational risk in addition to market and credit risk.

Pillar 2: Supervisory Review Process (SRP)—the establishment of suitable risk management systems in banks and their review by the supervisory authority.

Pillar 3: Market Discipline—increased transparency due to expanded disclosure requirements for banks.

The central focus of this framework as in Basel I, continues to be credit risk. In the revised framework, the minimum regulatory capital requirements take into account not just credit risk and market risk, but also operational risk. The measures for credit risk are more complex, for market risk they are the same, while those for operational risk are new. Besides, Basel II includes certain Pillar 2 risks such as credit concentration risks and liquidity risks.

Apart from an increase in the number of risks, banks are required to achieve a more comprehensive risk management framework. While Basel I required lenders to calculate a minimum level of capital based on a single risk weight for each of the limited number of asset classes, the capital requirements are more risk sensitive under Basel II. The credit risk weights are related directly to the credit rating of each counterparty instead of the counterparty category.

Basel II capital adequacy rules are based on a *menu* approach that allows differences in approaches in relationship to the nature of banks and the nature of markets in which they operate. The minimum requirements for the advanced approaches are technically more demanding and require extensive databases and more sophisticated risk management techniques. Basel II prescriptions have ushered in a transition from capital adequacy to capital efficiency which implies that banks adopt a more dynamic use of capital, in which capital will flow quickly to its most efficient uses. Unlike Basel I, Basel II is quite complex as it offers choices, some of which involve application of quantitative techniques.

The revised framework is designed to provide options to banks and banking systems for determining the capital requirements for credit risk, market risk and operational risk. It enables banks/supervisors to select approaches that are most appropriate for their operations and financial markets. The revised framework is expected to promote adoption of stronger risk management practices in banks. Under Basel II, capital requirements of banks will be more closely aligned with the underlying risks in the balance sheets of banks.

Operational Risk: One of the important features of the revised framework is the emphasis on operational risk. Operational risk is defined as the risk of loss resulting from inadequate or failed internal processes, people and systems or from external events. This definition includes legal risk, but excludes strategic and reputational risks. Operational risk differs from other banking risks in that it is typically not directly taken in return for an expected reward but is implicit in the ordinary course of corporate activity and has the potential to affect the risk management process. The Basel Committee identified the following seven types of operational risk events that have the potential to result in substantial losses.

1. Internal fraud.
2. External fraud.
3. Employment practices and workplace safety.
4. Clients, products and business practices.
5. Damage to physical assets.
6. Business disruption and system failures.
7. Execution, delivery and process management.

The potential losses, in turn, vary according to the business line within the bank in which the event occurs.

Management of specific operational risks is not new. It has

always been important for banks to try to prevent fraud, maintain the integrity of internal controls, reduce errors in transaction processing and so on. However, what is relatively new is the thrust on operational risk management as a comprehensive practice comparable to the management of credit risk and market risk. To manage operational risk, banks are gradually gearing to develop risk assessment techniques that are appropriate to the size and complexities of portfolios, their resources and data availability.

Implementation of Basel Norms in India: India has been adopting international best practices in the area of regulation and supervision with a view to strengthening the banking sector. Following the Basel Accord of 1988, the capital to risk-weighted assets ratio (CRAR)—which took into account the element of risk involved in both balance sheet as well as off-balance sheet business—emerged as a well-recognised and universally accepted measure of soundness of the banking system. Accordingly, as a part of banking sector reforms, India adopted the Basel norms in a phased manner. In fact, India went a step further and stipulated CRAR at 9 percent as against the international norm of 8 percent. Furthermore, India also prescribed the capital charge for market risk in June 2004, broadly in line with the 1996 amendment to Basel norms.

In order to ensuring migration to Basel II in a non-disruptive manner, given the complexities involved, a consultative approach was followed. The RBI released draft guidelines for implementation of Basel II in India on February 15, 2005. In terms of the draft guidelines, banks were required to adopt standardised approach for credit risk and basic indicator approach for operational risk. The standardised duration method would continue to be applied to arrive at the capital charge for market risk. Banks would need the RBI's approval for migration to advanced approaches of risk measurement.

With a view to ensuring smooth transition to the revised framework and providing opportunity to banks to streamline their systems and strategies, banks were required to commence a parallel run of the revised framework with effect from April 1, 2006. All scheduled commercial banks (except regional rural banks) were required to implement the revised capital adequacy framework with effect from March 31, 2007. However, Basel II framework in India became fully operational from end-March 2009.

Several measures were undertaken by the RBI to prepare the banking system to make a smooth migration to Basle II. Following the amendment to the Banking Companies (Acquisition and Transfer of Undertakings) Act in 1994, several public sector banks (PSBs) have raised capital both in India and abroad through Global Depository Receipts (GDRs). Several PSBs have also raised subordinated debt through the private placement. Concurrently, a series of regulatory initiatives were taken by the RBI relevant for Basel II.

First, concerted efforts were made to ensure that the banks had suitable risk management framework oriented towards their requirements, dictated by the size and complexity of business, risk philosophy, market perceptions and the expected level of capital. Second, Risk Based Supervision (RBS) was introduced in 23 banks on a pilot basis. Third, the RBI encouraged the banks to formalise their Internal Capital Adequacy Assessment Programme (ICAAP) in alignment with their business plans and performance budgeting system. Fourth, there has been a marked improvement in the area of disclosures, so as to have greater transparency in the financial position and risk profile of banks. Similarly, capacity building for ensuring the regulator's ability for identifying and permitting eligible banks to adopt Internal Ratings Based/Advanced Measurement approaches was given due priority.

The implementation of Basel II requires closer cooperation, information sharing and coordination of policies among sectoral supervisors, especially in the context of financial conglomerates.

Basis: In a futures market, basis is defined as the cash price (or spot price) of whatever is being traded minus its futures price for the contract in question. It is important because changes in the relationship between cash and futures prices affect the values of using futures as a hedge. A hedge, however, will always reduce risk as long as the volatility of the basis is less than the volatility of the price of whatever is being hedged.

Basis Point: One hundredth of a percentage point. Basis points are used in currency and bond markets where the size of trades mean that large amounts of money can change hands on small price movements. Thus if the yield on a financial instrument rises from 5.25 percent to 5.33 percent, the change is eight basis points.

Basis Risk: The risk that the relationship between the prices of a security and the instrument used to hedge it will change, thereby reducing the effectiveness of the hedge. In other words, it is the risk of varying fluctuations of the spot and the futures price between the moment at which a position is opened and the moment at which it is closed.

Bear: A pessimist market operator who expects the market price of shares to decline. The term also refers to the one who has sold shares which he does not possess, in the hope of buying them back at a lower price, when the market price of the shares come down in the near future.

Bearer Bonds: See Bearer Securities, *23*.

Bear Hug: A variety of takeover strategy that seeks to hurry target company managements to recommend acceptance of a tender offer in a short period of time.

Bear Market: A weak or falling market characterized by the dominance of sellers.

Bear Trap: A false signal indicating that the rising trend of a stock or index has reversed when in fact it has not. This can occur during a bear market reversal when short sellers believe the markets will sink back to its declining ways. If the market continues to rise, the shorters get trapped and are forced to cover their position at higher prices.

Bearer Securities: These are securities (or bonds) which do not require registration of the name of the owner in the books of the company. Both the interest and the principal whenever they become due are paid to anyone who has possession of the securities. No endorsement is required for changing the ownership of such securities.

Bench Mark: Security used as the basis for interest rate calculations and for pricing other securities. Also denotes the most heavily traded and liquid security of a particular class.

Benchmark Index: Indicators used to provide a point of reference for evaluating a fund's performance.

Beneficial Owner: The true owner of a security. Registered holder of the shares may act as a nominee to the true shareholders/owners.

Beta: It is a measure of the volatility of a stock relative to the market index in which the stock is included. A low beta indicates relatively low risk, a high beta indicates a high risk.

Bid: An offer of a price to buy as in an auction. Business on the stock exchange is done through bids. Bid also refers to the price one is willing to pay for a security.

Bid Spread: The difference between the stated and/or displayed price at which a market maker is willing to sell a security and the price at which he is willing to buy it.

Bilateral Netting: An arrangement between two parties in which they exchange only the net difference in their obligations to each other. The primary purpose of netting is to reduce exposure to credit/settlement risk.

Black Money: The term black money stands for money earned by illegal means and kept secretly and unaccounted for. It is widely used for smuggling activities, hoarding of scarce commodities (for purposes of speculation, profiteering and black marketing), bribing government officials, financing political activities, and ostentatious living. Secret business deals through black money in turn lead to tax evasion and a vicious circle is created in which one evil thrives on the other.

Black-Scholes Model: See Options, *158*.

Blank Transfer: Where the name of the transferee is left blank on share transfer form, it constitutes a blank transfer. A person depositing shares with a stock broker for immediate or eventual sale, has to sign a blank transfer form. It is also done when shares are mortgaged, so that in the event of non-payment the mortgager can fill in his own name in the transferee column and sell the share.

Block Trading: Buying and selling a block of securities usually takes place when restructuring or liquidating a large portfolio.

Blow Out: A security offering that sells out almost immediately.

Blue Chip: A highly rated share in terms of yield, safety, marketability and liquidity.

Board for Regulation and Supervision of Payment and Settlement Systems (BPSS): In order to provide focused attention to the payment and settlement systems, the RBI constituted the BPSS as a Committee of its Central Board. The Reserve Bank of India (Board for Regulation and Supervision of Payment and Settlement Systems) Regulations, 2005 were notified in the Gazette of India on February 18, 2005. The BPSS is headed by the Governor of the RBI with the Deputy Governor in-charge of Payment and Settlement Systems as the Vice-Chairman and the other Deputy Governors and two members of the Central Board of the RBI as members. The Executive Directors in-Charge of the Department of Payments and Settlement Systems (DPSS) and Financial Market Committee and Legal Adviser-in-Charge are permanent invitees. The Board also has an external expert as a permanent invitee. Functions and powers of the BPSS include the following.

1. Formulating policies relating to the regulation and supervision of all types of payment and settlement systems.
2. Setting standards for existing and future systems.
3. Authorising the payment and settlement systems.
4. Determining criteria for membership.

The National Payments Council, which was set up in 1999, has been designated as a Technical Advisory Committee of the BPSS. To assist the BPSS in performing its functions, a new department, the Department of Payments and Settlement Systems (DPSS), was set up in the RBI in March 2005.

Bombay Stock Exchange (BSE): BSE is a stock exchange located on Dalal Street, Mumbai. It was the 11th largest stock exchange in the world by market capitalisation as on December 31, 2012. Established in 1875, BSE Ltd. (formerly known as Bombay Stock Exchange Ltd.), is India's second oldest stock exchange (Oldest being the Calcutta Stock Exchange located at Lyons Range, Kolkata) and one of India's leading exchange groups.

In August 31, 1957, the BSE became the first stock exchange to be recognized by the Indian Government under the Securities Contracts Regulation Act. In 1980 the exchange moved to the Phiroze Jeejeebhoy Towers at Dalal Street, Fort area. In 1986 it developed the BSE SENSEX index, giving the BSE a means to measure overall performance of the exchange. In 2000 the BSE used this index to open its derivatives market, trading SENSEX futures contracts. The development of SENSEX options along with equity derivatives followed in 2001 and 2002, expanding the BSE's trading platform.

BSE has facilitated the growth of the Indian corporate sector by providing it an efficient capital-raising platform. BSE is a corporatized and demutualised entity, with a broad chorholder-base which includes two leading global exchanges, Deutsche Bourse, Fuse and Singapore Exchange as strategic partners. BSE provides an efficient and transparent market for trading in equity, debt instruments, derivatives, mutual funds. It also has a platform for trading in equities of small-and-medium enterprises (SME). More than 5,000 companies are listed on BSE making it world's Number 1 exchange in terms of listed members. BSE is world's fifth most active exchange in terms of number of transactions handled through its electronic trading system. It was also one of the world's leading exchanges (5th largest in December 2013) for index options trading (Source: World Federation of Exchanges).

BSE also provides a host of other services to capital market participants including risk management, clearing, settlement, market data services and education. It has a global reach with customers around the world and a nation-wide presence. BSE systems and processes are designed to safeguard market integrity, drive the growth of the Indian capital market and stimulate innovation and competition across all market segments. BSE is the first exchange in India and second in the world to obtain an ISO 9001:2000 certification. It is also the first exchange in the country and second in the world to receive Information Security Management System Standard BS 7799-2-2002 certification for its On-Line Trading System (BOLT).

It operates one of the most respected capital market educational institutes in the country (the BSE Institute Ltd.). BSE also provides depository services through its Central Depository Services Ltd. (CDSL) arm.

BSE's popular equity index—the S&P BSE SENSEX (formerly SENSEX)—is India's most widely tracked stock market benchmark index. It is traded internationally on the EUREX as well as leading exchanges of the BRICS nations (Brazil, Russia,

India, China and South Africa). On February 19, 2013, BSE entered into Strategic Partnership with S&P DOW JONES INDICES and the SENSEX was renamed as S&P BSE SENSEX.

Historically, an open outcry floor trading exchange, the BSE switched to an electronic trading system in 1995. This automated, screen-based trading platform is called BSE On-line Trading (BOLT). The BSE has also introduced the world's first centralized exchange-based internet trading system, BSEWEBx.co.in to enable investors anywhere in the world to trade on the BSE platform. See also National Stock Exchange of India Limited (NSE).

Bond: A negotiable certificate evidencing indebtedness issued by a company, municipality or government agency. A bond investor lends money to the issuer and, in exchange, the issuer promises to repay the loan amount on a specified maturity date. The issuer usually pays the bondholder periodic interest payments over the life of the loan.

Bonus Shares: Shares issued by companies to their shareholders free of cost by capitalization of accumulated reserves from the profits earned in the earlier years.

Book Building: It is a process by which a demand for the securities proposed to be issued by a corporate body is elicited and built up and the price for such securities is assessed for the determination of the quantum of such securities to be issued by means of a notice, circular, advertisement, document or information memoranda or offer document.

Book Closure: The periodic closure of the register of members and transfer books of the company, to take a record of the shareholders to determine their entitlement to dividends or to bonus or right shares or any other rights pertaining to shares.

Book Runner: A lead merchant banker who has been appointed by the issuer company for maintaining the book. The name of the book running lead manager is mentioned in the offer document of the issuer company.

Book Value: The net amount shown in the books or in the accounts for any asset, liability or owners' equity item. In the case of a fixed asset, it is equal to the cost or revalued amount of the asset less accumulated depreciation. The book value of a firm is its total net assets, i.e. the excess of total assets over total liabilities.

Boom: A condition of the market denoting increased activity with rising prices and higher volume of business resulting from greater demand of securities. It is a state where enlarged business, both investment and speculative, takes place for a sufficiently long period of time.

Breadth of the Market: The number of securities listed on the market in which there is regular trading.

Break: A rapid and sharp decline in a security or index.

Break-even Point: The stock price (or price) at which a particular strategy of transaction neither makes nor loses money. In options, the result is at the expiration date in the strategy. A dynamic break-even point changes as time passes.

Broker: A member of a stock exchange who acts as an agent for clients and buys and sells shares on their behalf in the market.

Broker Dealer: Any person, other than a bank, engaged in the business of buying or selling securities on its own behalf or for others.

Brokerage: Commission payable to the stockbroker for arranging sale or purchase of securities. Scale of brokerage is officially fixed by the stock exchange. Brokerage scales fixed in India are the maximum chargeable commission.

Bubble: A speculative sharp rise in share prices which like the bubble is expected to suddenly burst.

Bucketing: A situation where, in an attempt to make a short-term profit, a broker confirms an order to a client without actually executing it. If the eventual price that the order is executed at is higher than the price available when the order was submitted, the customer simply pays the higher price. On the other hand, if the execution price is lower than the price available when the order was submitted, the customer pays the higher price and the brokerage firm pockets the difference. It also means directly or indirectly taking the opposite side of client's order into the brokers own account or into an account in which the broker has interest, without open and competitive execution of the order on an exchange.

Bull: A market player who believes prices will rise and would, therefore, purchase a financial instrument with a view to selling it at a higher price. See also Bear.

Bull Market: A rising market with abundance of buyers and relatively few sellers.

Buoyancy: A rising trend in prices.

Business Day: A day on which the stock exchange is open for business and trading in securities.

Buy Back: The repurchase by a company of its own stock or bonds.

Buy on Margin: To buy shares with money borrowed from the stockbroker, who maintains a margin account for the customer.

Buyer of an Option: The buyer of an option is the one who by paying the option premium buys the right but not the obligation to exercise his option on the seller/writer.

Buying-in: When a seller fails to deliver shares to a buyer on the stipulated date, the buyer can enforce delivery by buying in against the seller in an auction.

Cc

Calendar Spread: The simultaneous sale and purchase of either calls or puts with the same strike price but different expiration months.

Call Money: The unpaid instalment of the share capital of a company, which a shareholder is called upon to pay.

Call Money Market: Money market in India comprises mainly of the call money market. Although other money market segments, viz. commercial bills market and inter-corporate deposits market have been in existence for a long time, there has not been much activity in these segments. Therefore, for assessing the impact of reforms on the money market, the focus is mainly on the call money market. The impact of reforms is assessed in terms of behaviour of the call money market and the market growth related parameters, including those instruments which were introduced in the 1990s.

Call money market deals in overnight funds. Notice money market deals in funds for 2 to 14 days. The call/notice money market serves the purpose of equilibrating the short-term liquidity position of banks and other participants. In order to modulate short-term liquidity under diverse market conditions, the Government introduced a full-fledged Liquidity Adjustment Facility (LAF) on June 5, 2000. Under this scheme, the RBI can adjust market liquidity on a daily basis through repo/reverse repo auctions of varying frequencies. This has emerged as an effective instrument to facilitate overnight call rate movement, resulting in stability and orderly market conditions.

Call Options: See Options, *158*.

Capital: It refers to: (a) equity shares, (b) fully, compulsorily and mandatorily convertible preference shares, and (c) fully, compulsorily and mandatorily convertible debentures.

Capital Account Transaction: A transaction which alters the assets or liabilities, including contingent liabilities, outside India of persons resident in India or assets or liabilities in India of persons resident outside India, and includes transactions referred to in sub-section (3) of Section 6 of Foreign Exchange Management Act (FEMA), 1999.

Capital Asset Pricing Model (CAPM): An economic theory that describes the relationship between risk and expected return and serves as a model for the pricing of risky securities. The CAPM asserts that the only risk that is priced by rational investors is systematic risk, because it cannot be eliminated by diversification. The CAPM says that the expected return of a security or a portfolio is equal to the rate on a risk-free security plus a risk premium.

Capital Market: Capital market is a market for long-term funds. The distinction between capital market and money market is not watertight. Broadly speaking, capital market focuses on financing of fixed investment (machinery and equipment) while money market provides working capital finance (raw material etc.).

Capital market channelises household savings to the corporate sector and allocates funds to firms. In this process, it allows both firms and households to share risks associated with business. Moreover, capital market enables the valuation of firms on an almost continuous basis and plays an important role in the governance of the corporate sector.

An efficient capital market is an important constituent of a sound financial system. In India, efforts have been made in recent years to set up an effective regulatory framework covering major participants in the capital market. Similarly, the technology of trading and settlements in the stock exchanges has been upgraded. Internet-based trading in securities has been permitted. Foreign institutional investors (FIIs) and pension funds were allowed to enter the Indian stock market from 1993 onwards. The market has undergone a major transformation in terms of its structure, products, practices, spread, institutional framework and other important aspects like transparency, integrity and efficiency since then. The size of the market has also grown manifold.

The capital market fosters economic growth in following ways:

1. It augments the quantum of savings and capital formation in the economy.
2. It allocates capital efficiently thereby raising the productivity of investment.
3. It enhances the efficiency of a financial system as diverse competitors vie with each other for financial resources.
4. It adds to the financial deepening of the economy by enlarging the financial sector and promoting the use of innovative, sophisticated and cost-effective financial instruments, which ultimately reduce the cost of capital.
5. Well-functioning capital markets also impose discipline on firms to perform.
6. Equity and debt markets stress on the banking sector by diversifying credit risk across the economy.

Capital Reserves: That portion of a company's profits which is not paid out as dividends to shareholders. They are also known as undistributable reserves and are ploughed back into the business.

Capital to Risk Weighted Assets Ratio (CRAR): CRAR is arrived at by dividing the capital of the bank with aggregated risk weighted assets for credit risk, market risk and operational risk. The higher the CRAR of a bank the better capitalized it is.

Carry Over Margin: The margin fixed by the stock exchange and payable by the members for carrying over the transactions from one settlement period to another.

Cash List: List of non-specified securities, traded usually for hand delivery and also for special delivery and spot delivery.

Cash Market: A market for sale of security against immediate delivery, as opposed to the futures market.

Cash Reserve Ratio (CRR): See Reserve Bank of India, *184*.

Cash Settlement: The settlement provision on some options and future contracts that do not require delivery of the underlying security. For options, the difference between the settlement price on the underlying asset and the option's exercise price is paid to the option holder at exercise. For future contracts, the exchange establishes a settlement price on the final day of trading and all remaining open positions are marked to market at that price.

Central Listing Authority: The authority set up to address the issue of multiple listing of the same security and to bring about uniformity in the due diligence exercise in scrutinising all listing applications on any stock exchanges. The functions include processing the application made by any body corporate, mutual fund or collective investment scheme for the letter of recommendation to get listed at the stock exchange, making recommendations as to listing conditions and any other functions as may be specified by SEBI from time to time.

Certificate of Deposit (CD): A negotiable certificate issued by a bank, usually for a period of one month to a year, as evidence of an interest bearing time deposit. This may also be offered at a discount.

CDs were introduced in 1989 as a money market instrument to mobilise large value deposits. Such deposits were freed from interest rate regulations in 1992. Banks can now have the option to meet their liquidity needs through these certificates issued at a premium during tight liquidity conditions.

CDs are essentially securitised short-term time deposits issued by banks during periods of tight liquidity, at relatively high interest rates (in comparison with term deposits). But the transaction cost of CDs is often lower as compared with that of retail deposits. When credit picks up, placing pressure on banks' liquidity, banks try to meet their liquidity gap by issuing CDs, often at a premium. The required amounts are mobilised in larger amounts through CDs, often for short periods in order to avoid interest liability overhang in the subsequent months when credit demand slackens. As banks offer higher interest rates on CDs, subscribers find it profitable to hold CDs till maturity. As a result, the secondary market for CDs has been slow to develop.

The steady increase of CDs has been on account of several factors.

1. Revised guidelines by the RBI on investments by banks in non-SLR debt securities.
2. Reduction in stamp duty on CDs effective March 1, 2004.
3. Withdrawal of tax deduction at source.
4. Disallowing premature closure of deposits under CDs.
5. Greater opportunity for secondary market trading.

On the demand side, the Securities and Exchange Board of India (SEBI) placing a bar on mutual funds (MFs) from parking funds in bank deposits coupled with improved funds position with MFs provided an impetus to the CD market. An encouraging development in the CD market is that some of the top-rated banks have been getting their CDs rated for better access to the market even when such rating is not mandatory under the extant guidelines.

Chalu Upla: Adjustment of position between two brokers either to avoid margin or to cross the trading or exposure limit.

Chinese Walls: Artificial barriers to the flow of information set up in large firms to prevent the movement of sensitive information between departments.

Churning: An unethical practice employed by some brokers to increase their commissions by excessively trading in a client's account. In the context of the stock market, churning refers to a period of heavy trading with few sustained price trends and little movement in stock market indices.

Circuit Breaker: A system to curb excessive speculation in the stock market, applied by the stock exchange authorities, when the index spurts or plunges by more than a specified percent. Trading is then suspended for some time to let the market cool down.

Circular Trading: A fraudulent trading scheme where sell or buy orders are entered by a person who knows that the same number of shares at the same time and for the same price either have been or will be entered. These trades do not represent a real change in the beneficial ownership of the security. These trades are entered with the intention of raising or depressing the prices of securities.

Clean Float: Where there is no official intervention and the price is permitted to vary in line with the market forces.

Clearing: Settlement or clearance of accounts, for a fixed period in a stock exchange.

Clearing Corporation of India Limited (CCIL): CCIL was incorporated on April 30, 2001 to provide clearing and settlement services in government securities, foreign exchange and money market instruments. The RBI took the initiative of setting up the CCIL with State Bank of India (SBI), Industrial Development Bank of India (IDBI), Life Insurance Corporation of India (LIC), ICICI Bank Ltd., Bank of Baroda and HDFC Bank Ltd. as its core promoters. This initiative was taken recognising the need for upgrading the country's financial infrastructure in respect of clearing and settlement of debt instruments and forex transactions. CCIL currently provides guaranteed settlement facility for government securities clearing, clearing of Collateralised Borrowing and Lending Obligations (CBLO) and foreign exchange clearing.

CCIL-operated systems include the following:

Government Securities Segment: During 1996-2002, a quasi-DvP system was in place with the book-entry system in government securities not directly linked with the funds accounts, with no mechanism to prevent a gridlock in the system. In 2002, CCIL was constituted by the banks to play the role of a CCP and for providing a settlement guarantee mechanism. The government securities settlement system has evolved since then and transactions are now settled on a net basis. Settlement through CCIL has the following advantages: (a) assurance of settlement to the members on the settlement date, (b) reduction in counterparty exposure, (c) operational efficiency, and (d) improved liquidity.

CCIL provides guaranteed settlement of all secondary market outright sales and repo transactions in government securities by the process of novation. All trades reported on the RBI's NDS platform or contracted on the online anonymous, trading plátform NDSOM, are accepted by CCIL for settlement after the necessary validations. These trades are settled on a DvP-III basis, i.e. the funds leg and the securities leg are settled on a net basis.

CBLO Segment: The CBLO is a money market product developed by CCIL and launched on January 20, 2003. The product was initially developed with a view to providing entities that have been phased out from the unsecured inter-bank call money market with an avenue for their funds operations. A repo variant, CBLO enables borrowing/lending of funds of various maturities up to one year, fully backed by collaterals in the form of central government securities/treasury bills. CCIL provides guaranteed settlement facility for trades in this instrument as a central counterparty. The funds leg of the trades in this instrument is settled in the current account maintained by these entities with the RBI. The borrowing and lending takes place through an electronic anonymous order matching platform. CBLO operates in a Straight-through Processing (STP)-enabled environment, seamlessly encompassing dealing to settlement.

The CBLO market has now become the preferred option for participants in the money market. The volume in this market is now significantly higher than the combined volumes in the call and the repo market.

Forex Segment: CCIL provides a guaranteed settlement facility for all US dollar-Indian Rupee inter-bank Cash, Tom, Spot and forward transactions. The matched and accepted forward deals are guaranteed for settlement from S-2 day (two days previous to settlement) and the Spot, Tom, Cash deals are guaranteed for settlement from the trade date as the CCIL becomes the central counterparty to every accepted trade through the process of novation. The rupee-leg of the transaction is settled through the member's current account with the RBI and the US dollar leg through CCIL's account with the Settlement Bank at New York.

CCIL also provides continuous-linked settlement (CLS) settlement services for banks in India by availing of third party services of a settlement bank. Banks participating in this segment of CCIL report their cross-currency trades to the settlement bank directly or through CCIL. The settlement is made through the nostro accounts of CCIL with the settlement bank in CLS settlement currencies.

The settlement of forex transactions by CCIL has resulted in a reduction in counterparty exposure, increased operational efficiency and overall lower operational costs. Forex settlement volumes in CCIL have been rising consistently through the years and have witnessed substantial growth since it commenced operations.

Clearing House: A department of an exchange or a separate legal entity that provides a range of services related to the clearance and settlement of trades and the management of risks associated with the resulting contracts. A clearing house is often central counterparty to all trades, i.e. the buyer to every seller and seller to every buyer.

Clearing Member: A member of a clearing corporation or clearing house of the derivatives exchange or derivatives segment of an exchange, who may clear and settle transactions in securities.

Close Out: A purchase or sale transaction leaving a trader with a zero net position.

Close-ended Fund: A type of investment company that has a fixed number of shares which are publicly traded. The price of a closed-end share fluctuates based on investor supply and demand. Closed-ended funds are not required to redeem shares and have managed portfolios.

Close-out-netting: An arrangement to settle all contracted but not yet due obligations to and claims on a counterparty by one single payment, immediately upon the occurrence of one of the defined events of default.

Closing Buy Transaction: Means a buy transaction which will have the effect of partly or fully offsetting a short position.

Closing Out: Where a party to a contract does not make delivery against sale or payment against delivery of documents, the other party can close out the transaction against the defaulting party. The gain or loss arising from the closing out is borne by the defaulter.

Closing Price: The rate at which the last transaction in a security is struck before the close of the trading hours.

Closing Sell Transaction: Means a sell transaction which will have the effect of partly or fully offsetting a long position.

Collateral: Assets that are offered to secure a loan or other credit. For example, if you get a real estate mortgage, the bank's collateral is typically your house. Collateral becomes subject to seizure on default.

Collateralised Borrowing and Lending Obligations (CBLO): It is a money market instrument as approved by the RBI. It is a product developed by Clearing Corporation of India Limited (CCIL) (q.v.) for the benefit of entities who have either been phased out from the inter-bank call money market or have been given restricted participation in terms of ceiling on call borrowing and lending transactions and who do not have access to the call money market. CBLO is a discounted instrument available in electronic book entry form for a maturity period ranging from one day to ninety days (can be made available up to one year as per guidelines of RBI).

CBLO is explained as under:

1. An obligation by the borrower to return the money borrowed, at a specified future date.
2. An authority to the lender to receive money lent, at a specified future date with an option/privilege to transfer the authority to another person for value received.
3. An underlying charge on securities held in custody (with CCIL) for the amount borrowed/lent.

Collateralised Mortgage Obligation (CMO): A generic term for a security backed by real estate mortgages. CMO payment obligations are covered by interest and/or principal payments from a pool of mortgages. In addition to its generic meaning, CMO usually suggest a non governmental issue.

Collective Investment Management Company: A company incorporated under the provisions of the Companies Act, 1956 and registered with SEBI under the SEBI (Collective Investment Schemes) Regulations, 1999, whose object is to organise, operate and manage a Collective Investment Scheme (q.v.).

Collective Investment Scheme (CIS): Any scheme or arrangement made or offered by any company under which the contributions, or payments made by the investors, are pooled and utilized with a view to receive profits, income, produce or property, and is managed on behalf of the investors is a CIS. Investors do not have day-to-day control over the management and operation of such scheme or arrangement.

Commercial Bill: It is a marketable instrument and an important device for providing short-term credit to business and industry. Commercial bills (or bills of exchange) are issued by business firms. Business firms often sell goods on credit and the buyers promise to pay the value of goods after a specified period of time, say 3 months. Thus, a bill with a maturity period of 3 months is like a post-dated cheque to be honoured by the buyer of goods. The holder of the bill may need cash before the maturity date and in that case he can sell it to some other person or to a bank at a discount. Bills are of two types: (a) demand bills which are payable on demand or presentation or sight as, for example, a bank draft, and (b) time bills which are payable after a stipulated time period, generally 3 months.

Commercial Paper (CP): A short-term promise to repay a fixed amount that is placed on the market either directly or through a specialized intermediary. It is usually issued by companies with a high credit standing in the form of a promissory note redeemable at par to the holder on maturity and therefore does not require any guarantee.

CP was introduced as a money market instrument in January 1990. The purpose was to enable the companies to diversify their sourcing of short-term borrowings. It also provided investors with an additional instrument for investment.

CP is issued by non-banking companies and All-India Financial Institutions (AIFIs) as an unsecured promissory note or in a dematerialised form at a rate of discount not tied to any transaction. It is privately placed with investors through the agency of banks. Banks act as both principals (i.e. as counter parties in purchases and sales) and agents in dealership and placement.

The pricing of CP usually lies between the scheduled commercial banks' lending rate and some representative money market rate. The Indian CP market is driven by the demand for CP by scheduled commercial banks, which in turn is governed by bank liquidity. Banks' investments in CP, despite a positive interest rate differential between the bank loan rate and the CP rate, may be explained by two factors, viz.: (i) the higher transaction costs of bank loans, and (ii) the relative profitability of CP as an attractive short-term instrument to park funds during times of high liquidity.

The Indian CP market is driven by swings in bank liquidity. Banks prefer investing in CPs especially in times of easy liquidity as they can park funds at interest rates higher than call rates and at the same time avoid higher transaction costs associated with bank loans. The effective discount rate of CP usually lies between representative money market rate and the bank lending rate. On the other hand, companies are able to raise funds through CPs at a lower rate than the lending rates of banks under easy liquidity conditions.

Common Stock: Units of ownership of a public corporation. Holders of common stock typically have voting rights and receive dividends, but there is no guarantee of dividend payment.

Competitive Bid: An offer made by a person other than the acquirer who has made the first public announcement.

Composite Issues: An issue of securities by a listed company on a public-cum-rights basis offered through a single offer document wherein the allotment for both public and rights component of the issue is proposed to be made simultaneously.

Compulsory Delisting: Permanent removal of securities of a listed company from a stock exchange as a penalizing measure at the behest of the stock exchange for not making submissions/complying with various requirements set out in the Listing agreement within the time frames prescribed.

Continuous Disclosure: Procedure where certain companies are required to make disclosures on a continuing basis of their business activities by filing documents.

Convergence: Narrowing of the difference between the futures contract and the value of the underlying asset during the final days of the contract.

Conversion Price: The price at which a convertible instrument is converted into shares of the company.

Conversion Ratio: The number of shares which may be acquired upon the conversion of a convertible instrument. The ratio is calculated as instrument's principal amount divided by conversion price.

Convertible Bond: A bond giving the investor the option to convert the bond into equity at a fixed conversion price or as per a pre-determined pricing formula.

Corporate Debt Market: In any country, companies face different types of financing choices at different stages of development. Reflecting the varied supplies of different types of capital and their costs, regulatory policies and financial innovations, the financing patterns of firms vary geographically and temporally. While developed countries rely more on market-based sources of finance, the developing countries rely more on bank-based sources. The development of a corporate bond market, for direct financing of the capital requirements of corporates by investors assumes paramount importance, particularly in a liberalised financial system.

Corporate debt market provides an alternative means of long-term resources to corporates—alternative to financing by banks and financial institutions. The size and growth of private corporate debt market depends upon several factors, including financing patterns of companies. Among market-based sources of financing, while the equity markets have been largely developed, the corporate bond markets in most developing countries have remained relatively underdeveloped. This has been the result of dominance of the banking system combined with the weaknesses in market infrastructure and inherent complexities. However, credit squeeze following the Asian financial crisis in the mid-1990s drew attention of policy makers to the importance of multiple financing channels in an economy. Alternative sources of finance, apart from banks, need to be actively developed to support higher levels of investment and economic growth. The development of corporate debt market has, therefore, become the prime concern of regulators in developing countries.

From the perspective of developing countries, a liquid corporate bond market can play a critical role in supporting economic development in the following ways:

1. It supplements the banking system to meet the requirements of the corporate sector for long-term capital investment and asset creation.
2. It provides a stable source of finance when the equity market is volatile.
3. With the decline in the role of specialised financial institutions, there is an increasing realisation of the need for a well-developed corporate debt market as an alternative source of finance.
4. Corporate bond markets can also help firms reduce their overall cost of capital by allowing them to tailor their asset and liability profiles to reduce the risk of maturity and currency mismatches.
5. Corporate bond market is important for nurturing a credit culture and market discipline.
6. The existence of a well-functioning bond market can lead to the efficient pricing of credit risk as expectations of all bond market participants are incorporated into bond prices.

Apart from providing a channel for financing investments, the corporate bond markets also contribute towards portfolio diversification for holders of long-term funds. Effective asset management requires a balance of asset alternatives. In view of the underdeveloped state of the corporate bond markets, there would be an overweight position in government securities and even equities. The existence of a well-functioning corporate bond market widens the array of asset choices for long-term investors such as pension funds and insurance companies and allows them to better manage the maturity structure of their balance sheets.

Corporate Debt Market in India: India is now one of the fastest growing economies in the world and is endeavouring to step up the growth rate. Limited availability of adequate long-term resources could adversely affect India's infrastructure development. Infrastructure financing requirements are large and could not be expected to be met by the banking sector alone. Banks already appear to have significant exposure to long-term funds. They may, therefore, not be in a position to fund long-term projects in future to the extent they have been able to do in recent years. Inadequate long-term resources could, therefore, act as a constraint on India's future growth prospects. In the absence of a well-functioning debt market, even large corporates fund their requirements from the banking system, limiting the availability of bank funds for small and medium enterprises and other sectors. This also raises the cost of borrowings for them. Thus, development of the capital market, in general, and the debt market, in particular, is crucial from the point of view of reducing corporate sector's reliance on the banking system so as to enable it to focus more on lending to small and medium enterprises, and agriculture and allied activities.

Corporates in India have traditionally relied heavily on borrowings from banks and financial institutions (FIs) to finance their investments. Equity financing has also been used, but largely during periods of surging equity prices. However, bond issuances by companies have remained limited in size and scope. Given the huge funding requirements, especially for long-term infrastructure projects, the corporate debt market has a crucial role to play and needs to be nurtured.

In India, banks and FIs have traditionally been the most important external sources of finance for the corporate sector. The second half of the 1980s saw some activity in primary bond issuances, but these were largely by the public sector undertakings (PSUs). The corporates relied more on banks for meeting short-term working capital requirements and DFIs for financing long-term investment. However, in view of the declining role of DFIs in recent years, a gap has appeared for long-term finance. Commercial banks have managed to fill this gap, but only to an extent as there are asset-liability mismatch issues for banks in providing longer-maturity credit.

In the 1990s, the equity market in India witnessed a series of reforms, which helped in bringing it on par with international standards. However, the corporate debt market has not been able to develop due to lack of market infrastructure and a comprehensive regulatory framework. For a variety of reasons, the issuers resorted to private placement of bonds as opposed to public issues of bonds.

Emergence of Private Placement Market: In private placement, resources are raised privately through arrangers (merchant banking intermediaries) who place securities with a limited number of investors such as financial institutions, corporates and high net worth individuals. Under Section 81 of the Companies Act, 1956, a private placement is defined as 'an issue of shares or of convertible securities by a company to a select group of persons'. An offer of securities to more than 50 persons is deemed to be a public issue under the Act. Corporates access the private placement market because of its following advantages:

1. It is a cost and time-effective method of raising funds.
2. It can be structured to meet the needs of the entrepreneurs.

Private placement does not require detailed compliance of formalities as required in public or rights issues.

The emergence of private placement market has provided an easier alternative to the corporates to raise funds. Although the private placement market provides a cost-effective and time-saving mechanism for raising resources, the unbridled growth of this market has raised some concerns. The quality of issues and extent of transparency in the private placement deals remain areas of concern even though privately placed issues by listed companies are now required to be listed and also subject to necessary disclosures. In the case of public issues, all the issues coming to the market are screened for their quality and the investors rely on ratings and other public information for evaluation of risk. Such a screening mechanism is missing in the case of private placements. This increases the risk associated with privately placed securities. Further, the private placement market appears to be growing at the expense of the public issues market, which has some distinct advantages in the form of wider participation by the investors and, thus, diversification of the risk.

The private placement market was not regulated until May 2004. In view of the mushrooming growth of the market and the risk posed by it, SEBI prescribed that the listing of all debt securities, irrespective of the mode of issuance, i.e. whether issued on a private placement basis or through public/rights issue, shall be done through a separate listing agreement. The RBI also issued guidelines to the financial intermediaries under its purview on investments in non-SLR securities, including private placement. In June 2001, boards of banks were advised to lay down policy and prudential limits on investments in bonds and debentures, including cap on unrated issues and on a private placement basis. The policy laid down by banks should prescribe stringent appraisal of issues, especially by non-borrower customers, provide for an internal system of rating, stipulate entry-level minimum ratings/quality standards and put in place proper risk management systems.

Corporate Debt Restructuring: A Special Group (Chairperson: Smt. S. Gopinath) was appointed by RBI to undertake a further review of the corporate debt restructuring (CDR) mechanism and suggest certain changes/improvements in the existing scheme for enhancing its scope and to make it more efficient. In pursuance of the recommendations made by the Special Group, major modifications were proposed in the draft guidelines issued on May 6, 2005 in the existing CDR scheme which included the following.

1. Extension of scheme to corporate entities where banks and institutions have an outstanding exposure of ₹ 10 crore or more from the earlier exposure of ₹ 20 crore and above.
2. Requirement of support of 60 percent of creditors by number in addition to the support of 75 percent of creditors by value with a view to making the decision-making process more

equitable.

3. Linking the restoration of asset classification prevailing on the date of reference to CDR Cell for implementation of package within three months from the date of approval of the package.
4. Restricting the regulatory concession in asset classification and provisioning requirement to the first restructuring where the package also has to meet certain norms relating to turnaround period and minimum sacrifice and funds infusion by promoters.
5. Convergence in the methodology for computation of economic sacrifice among banks and FIs.
6. Regulatory treatment of non-SLR instruments acquired while funding interest or in *lieu* of outstanding principal and valuation of such instruments.
7. Limiting the RBI's role to providing broad guidelines for the CDR system.
8. Enhancing balance sheet disclosures.
9. Pro-rata sharing of additional finance requirement.
10. Including one-time settlement (OTS) as part of the CDR scheme to make the exit option more flexible.
11. Discretion to the core group in dealing with wilful defaulters in certain cases.

Corporate Governance: The way in which companies run themselves, in particular the way in which they are accountable to those who have a vested interest in their performance, especially their shareholders.

Coupon: The interest paid on a bond expressed as a percentage of the face value. If a bond carries a fixed coupon, the interest is paid on an annual or semi-annual basis. The term also describes the detachable certificate entitling the bearer to payment of the interest.

Coupon Rate: The interest rate stated on the face of Coupon (q.v.).

Coverage Ratio: Equity minus net NPAs (non-performing assets) divided by total assets minus intangible assets.

Credit Cards: There has been phenomenal increase in the number of credit cards issued by the banks in India during the last few years.

While the increasing usage of the credit cards is a welcome development in as much as it reduces reliance on currency for settlement of transactions, it also entails certain additional elements of operational risk and can be a potential source of customer complaints. RBI, based on the complaints received from the credit card holders, had undertaken a study of the credit card operations of the banks. The recommendations emerging from the study were communicated to the banks in July 2008, for implementation. These recommendations are fairly wide-ranging and encompass several issues in the following areas:

1. Card issuance.
2. Card statements.
3. Interest and other chares on the cards.
4. Using the services of direct selling/marketing agents.
5. Redressal of grievances of customers.
6. Reporting of default information of the card holder to the CIBIL.

Credit Default Swap (CDS): See Credit Derivatives, *49*.

Credit Derivatives: The credit derivatives are gaining increasing popularity in many countries. Since the early 1990s, there has been proliferation of different types of credit derivatives in several countries.

A credit derivative is a contract (derivative) to transfer the risk of the total return on a credit asset falling below an agreed level, without transfer of the underlying asset. This is usually achieved by transferring risk on a credit reference asset. Early forms of credit derivatives were financial guarantees. Credit derivatives are designed to allow independent trading/hedging of credit risk. It is also possible to transfer and/or transform credit risk through securitisation. Credit derivative is a logical extension of two of the most significant developments in financial markets, *viz.* securitisation and derivatives.

Forms of Credit Derivatives: Credit derivatives are instruments that transfer a part or all of the credit risk of an obligation (or a pool of obligations), without transferring the ownership of the underlying asset(s). This is usually achieved by transferring risk on a credit reference asset. Three common forms of credit derivatives are credit default swap (CDS), total return swap (TRS) and credit linked note (CLN).

A. Credit Default Swap (CDS): A CDS consists of swapping, usually on an ongoing basis, the risk premium inherent in an interest rate on a bond or a loan in return for a cash payment that is made in the event of default by the debtor. The CDS has become the main driver of the credit derivatives market, offering liquid price discovery and trading on which the rest of the market is based. It is an agreement between a protection buyer and a protection seller, whereby the buyer pays a periodic fee in return for a contingent payment by the seller upon a credit event happening in the reference entity. The contingent payment usually replicates the loss incurred by creditor of the reference entity in the event of its default. It covers only the credit risk embedded in the asset, risks arising from other factors, such as interest rate movements, remain with the buyer.

B. Total Return Swap (TRS): A TRS (also known as total rate of return swap) is a contract between two counterparties, whereby they swap periodic payments for the period of the contract. Typically, one party receives the total return (interest payments plus any capital gains or losses for the payment period) from a specified reference asset, while the other receives a specified fixed or floating cash flow that is not related to the creditworthiness of the reference asset, as with a vanilla interest rate swap. The payments are based upon the same notional amount. The reference asset may be any asset, index or basket of assets. The TRS is simply a mechanism that allows one party to derive the economic benefit of owning an asset without use of the balance sheet, and which allows the other to effectively buy protection against loss in value due to ownership of a credit assets.

While the CDS provides protection against specific credit events, the TRS protects against the loss of value irrespective of cause, whether default and widening of credit spreads, among others.

C. Credit Linked Note (CLN): A CLN is an instrument whose cash flow depends upon a credit event, which can be a default, credit spread, or rating change. The definition of the relevant credit events must be negotiated by the parties to the note. A CLN, in effect, combines a credit-default swap with a regular note (with coupon, maturity, redemption). Given its regular-note features, a CLN is an on-balance sheet asset, unlike a CDS.

Significance of Credit Derivatives: Credit derivative markets are most active where credit quality measurement and rating systems are transparent and have widespread adoption as in North America and Europe. In addition, the demand for structured credit products in Asia and the Middle East has been growing. The rapid pace of growth and widespread participation in the credit derivatives market in several countries has transformed the financial landscape. Credit derivatives have significance for both banks and investors in mitigating credit risk. For instance, a commercial bank can use credit derivatives to manage the risk of its loan portfolio and an investment bank can use credit derivatives to manage the risks it incurs when underwriting securities. Investors—such as an insurance company, asset manager, or hedge fund—can use credit derivatives to align its credit risk exposure with its desired credit risk profile.

Credit derivatives in international markets have effectively helped to enhance the efficiency of the financial system by providing to both bank and non-bank financial institutions access to a broader range of risk-return combinations and a wider pool of underlying risks and enhancing the liquidity of corporate bond markets. The information revealed through credit derivative mechanism is very useful for supervision and market surveillance.

Benefits of Credit Derivatives: Banks and the financial institutions derive at least three main benefits from credit derivatives:

Credit derivatives allow banks to transfer credit risk and hence free up capital, which can be used for other productive purposes.

Banks can conduct business on existing client relationships in excess of exposure norms and transfer away the risks. For instance, a bank which has hit its exposure limits with a client group may have to turn down a lucrative guarantee deal. However, with credit derivatives, the bank can take up the guarantee and maintain its exposure limits by transferring the credit risk on the guarantee or previous exposures. This allows banks to maintain client relationships.

Banks can construct and manage a credit risk portfolio of their own choice and risk appetite unconstrained by funds, distribution and sales effort.

Risks Involved in Credit Derivatives: Credit derivatives pose risk management challenges of their own. Credit derivatives can transform credit risk in intricate ways that may not be easy to understand. Complex credit derivatives rely on complex models, leading to model risk. Credit rating agencies interpret this complexity for investors, but their ratings can be misunderstood, creating rating agency risk. The settlement of a credit derivative contract following a default can have its own complications, creating settlement risk.

Apart from these risks, the credit risk remains the core risk in the credit derivative segment. The use of credit derivative instruments has changed the underlying borrower-lender relationship and established new relationships between lenders that become risk shedders and the new risk takers. This new relationship has the potential for market failure due, for instance, to asymmetric information. The growth of hedge funds, particularly credit-oriented hedge funds, has accelerated market development and credit risk dispersion. While credit derivative markets increasingly facilitate the primary transfer of credit risk, secondary market liquidity is still lacking within some segments, creating the potential for market disruptions. As such, these markets are subject to increased attention from supervisors and policymakers and raise some supervisory concerns.

In short, the use of credit derivatives raises the following concerns:

1. Some of the credit derivatives, which are being used, are at their infancy and need to mature. Introduction of such products, therefore, may be potentially destabilising.
2. The measurement and management of credit risk is much more complicated than market risk.
3. Documentation risk is an important aspect of credit derivatives.

Certain incentive issues arise with the use of credit derivatives. This is because such instruments typically change the underlying borrower-lender relationship and establish new relationships between lenders that become risk shedders and the new risk takers. This new relationship has the potential for market failure due, for instance, to asymmetric information. See also Financial Derivatives.

Credit Information Bureau (India) Limited [CIBIL]: Set up in 2000, it provides a vital service, which allows its members to make informed, objective and faster credit decisions. CIBIL's aim is to fulfil the need of credit granting institutions for comprehensive credit information by collecting, collating and disseminating credit information pertaining to both commercial and consumer borrowers, to a closed user group of members. Banks, financial institutions, non-banking financial companies, housing finance companies and credit card companies use CIBIL's services. Data sharing is based on the principle of reciprocity, which means that only members who have submitted all their credit data, may access Credit Information Reports from CIBIL.

With a view to strengthening the legal mechanism and facilitating credit information companies to collect, process and share credit information on borrowers of banks/FIs, a draft Credit Information Companies (Regulation) Bill was passed in May 2005 and notified in June 2005. The Government and the Reserve

Bank have framed rules and regulations for implementation of the Act, with specific provisions for protecting individual borrower's rights and obligations. The rules and regulations were notified on December 14, 2006. In terms of the provisions of the Act, after obtaining the certificate of registration from the Reserve Bank to commence/carry on business of credit information companies will be able to collect all types of credit information (positive as well as negative) from their member credit institutions and disseminate the same in the form of credit reports to the specified users/individuals.

Credit Linked Note (CLN): See Credit Derivatives, *49*.

Credit Rating: Credit ratings measure a borrower's creditworthiness and provide an international framework for comparing the credit quality of issuers and rated debt securities. Rating agencies allocate three kinds of ratings: issuer credit ratings, long-term debt, and short-term debt. Issuer credit ratings are amongst the most widely watched. They measure the creditworthiness of the borrower including its capacity and willingness to meet financial needs. The top credit rating issued by the main agencies—Standard & Poor's, Moody's and Fitch IBCA—is AAA or Aaa. This is reserved for a few sovereign and corporate issuers. Ratings are divided into two broad groups - investment grade and speculative (junk) grade.

Credit Rating in India: Credit-rating in India is relatively new, compared to the developed economies. The first rating agency, CRISIL, was set up in 1987. Credit-rating was made mandatory for commercial papers and debentures from 1991—when ICRA, India's second credit-rating agency was established. Since then, the rating industry has grown significantly in terms of rated debt issued and subscribed, both at the corporate and retail levels (primarily fixed deposits).

The importance of credit rating agencies in India as information providers, which had been increasing, came to greater focus with the adoption of Basel II framework. The rating agencies in India face two constraints which impact their default statistics. One; they have a small base of rated entities. Two, they lack the geographical diversification benefits which the international rating entities enjoy. The processes and methodologies adopted by rating agencies in India are generally in alignment with those of the international rating agencies. Moreover, despite the above two constraining factors, their default statistics may not be out of sync with the Basel trigger ratios. The domestic rating agencies are equipped to scale up their resources, when required, to cater to a higher demand for ratings consequent upon implementation of Basel II.

At present, the ratings in India are issue-specific and not issuer-specific. The rating agencies, therefore, are also working out methodologies for undertaking issuer ratings. It is, therefore, expected that with the implementation of Basel II in India, the proportion of rated entities is likely to increase over a period, providing the appropriate basis for risk discrimination in the system.

Credit Rating Agency: Credit rating agency means a body corporate which is engaged in, or proposes to be engaged in, the business of rating of securities offered by way of public or rights issue.

Credit Risk: The risk that a party to a contractual agreement or transaction will be unable to meet its obligations or will default on commitments. Credit risk can be associated with almost any financial transaction. Basel-II provides two options for measurement of capital charge for credit risk:

1. **Standardised Approach (SA):** Under the SA, the banks use a risk-weighting schedule for measuring the credit risk of its assets by assigning risk weights based on the rating assigned by the external credit rating agencies.
2. **Internal Rating Based Approach (IRB):** The IRB approach, on the other hand, allows banks to use their own internal ratings of counterparties and exposures, which permit a finer differentiation of risk for various exposures and hence delivers capital requirements that are better aligned to the degree of risks. The IRB approaches are of two types:

- **Foundation IRB (FIRB):** The bank estimates the Probability of Default (PD) associated with each borrower, and the supervisor supplies other inputs such as Loss Given Default (LGD) and Exposure at Default (EAD).
- **Advanced IRB (AIRB):** In addition to Probability of Default (PD), the bank estimates other inputs such as EAD and LGD. The requirements for this approach are more exacting. The adoption of advanced approaches would require the banks to meet minimum requirements relating to internal ratings at the outset and on an ongoing basis such as those relating to the design of the rating system, operations, controls, corporate governance, and estimation and validation of credit risk components, viz., PD for both FIRB and AIRB and LGD and EAD for AIRB. The banks should have, at the minimum, PD data for five years and LGD and EAD data for seven years. In India, banks have been advised to compute capital requirements for credit risk adopting the SA.

Credit Risk Mitigation: Techniques used to mitigate the credit risks through exposure being collateralised in whole or in part with cash or securities or guaranteed by a third party.

Cross Collateralization: Practice of using assets as back up or secondary collateral for debt other than the debt they are primarily pledged for. A network of cross collateralization may facilitate an increase in borrowing or a reduction in borrowing cost.

Cross-Rate: The exchange rate between currencies A and C which is derived from the rate between A and B and the rate between B and C. Thus, if US$ 1 = ₹ 60 and US$ 1 = Yen 240, the cross rate between ₹ and Yen is ₹ 1 = Yen 4.

Cum: Means *with.* A cum price includes the right to any declared dividend (cum dividend) or bonus (cum bonus).

Cumulative Convertible Preference Shares: A type of

preference shares where the dividend payable on the same accumulates, if not paid. After a specified date, these shares are converted into equity capital of the company.

Cumulative Preference Shares: A type of preference shares on which dividend accumulates if not paid. All arrears of preference dividend have to be paid out before paying dividend on equity shares.

Current Ratio: Current ratio measures a company's current assets relative to its current liabilities. This gives an indication of its abilities to meet short-term liabilities; the higher the ratio, the more liquid the company.

Custodian: An organization, usually a bank or any other approved institution that holds the securities and other assets of mutual funds and other institutional investors.

Custody Risk: The risk of loss of securities held in custody occasioned by the insolvency, negligence or fraudulent action of the custodian or of a sub-custodian.

Dd

Dabba Trading: Trading of securities outside the stock exchange. The broker, instead of routing the trade of his clients in the system of stock exchanges, matches or executes the trades of its clients in a system provided by him outside the stock exchange.

Daily Margin: The amount that has to be deposited at the stock exchange on a daily basis for the purchase or sale of a security. This amount is decided by the stock exchange.

Daisy Chain: A kind of fictitious trading, or wash selling, whereby a group of unscrupulous investors artificially inflate the price of a security so that they sell it at a profit. As a stock price rises due to increased volume, innocent investors may be attracted to the stock in order to participate in the rising price. These investors are typically caught owning a stock that continues to depreciate long after the daisy chain sells out their positions for a profit.

Dalal Street: Street in Mumbai on which Bombay Stock Exchange (BSE) is situated.

Data Confidentiality: Protection of data from unauthorized disclosure is called data confidentiality. Due to the open nature of Internet, unless otherwise protected, all data transfer can be monitored or read by others. Although it is difficult to monitor a transmission at random, because of numerous paths available, special programmes such as *sniffers*, set up at an opportune location like web server, can collect vital information. This may include credit card numbers, deposits, loans or passwords etc. Confidentiality extends beyond data transfer and includes any connected data storage system including network storage systems. Passwords and other access control methods help in ensuring data confidentiality.

Data Dissemination: It refers to all the means by which data are made available to the public, including dissemination on the Internet.

Data Integrity: It ensures that information cannot be modified in unexpected way. Loss of data integrity could result from human error, intentional tampering, or even catastrophic events. Failure to protect the correctness of data may render data useless, or worse, dangerous. Efforts must be made to ensure the accuracy and soundness of data at all times. Access control, encryption and digital signatures are the methods to ensure data integrity.

Dawn Raid: A situation in which a predator broker sweeps into the market the instant it opens and buys up a large block of shares before the others have chance to react.

Day Order: A day order, as the name suggests, is an order which is valid for the day on which it is entered. If the order is not executed during the day, the system cancels the order automatically at the end of the day.

Dealer: A firm that enters into transactions as a counterparty on both sides of the market in one or more products.

Debentures: Bonds issued by a company bearing a fixed rate of interest usually payable half yearly on specific dates and principal amount repayable on a particular date on redemption of the debentures.

Debentures represent creditorship securities and debentures holders are long-term creditors of the company. As a secured instrument, it is a promise to pay interest and repay principal at stipulated times.

The payment of interest and repayment of principal is a contractual obligation enforceable by law. Failure/default leads to bankruptcy of the company. The claim of debenture holders on income and assets ranks pari passu with other secured debt and higher than that of shareholders—preference as well as ordinary shares.

Convertible debentures give the holders the right (option) to convert them into equity shares on certain terms. They are entitled to a fixed income till the conversion option is exercised and share the benefits associated with equity shares after the conversion.

Debit Card: A debit card allows the account owner to access his funds electronically. Debit cards may be used to obtain cash from automated teller machines or purchase goods or services using point-of-sale systems. The use of a debit card involves immediate debiting and crediting of consumers' accounts.

Debt Recovery Tribunals: Debt Recovery Tribunals (DRTs) were set up under the Recovery of Debts Due to Banks and Financial Institutions Act, 1993 for expeditious adjudication and recovery of debts due to banks and financial institutions. On the recommendation of the RBI, the Government of India set up a Working Group in July 2004 to improve the functioning of DRTs. The Working Group is to examine issues and recommend appropriate measures regarding: (a) the need to extend the provisions of the Recovery of Debts Due to Banks and Financial Institutions Act to cases for less than ₹ 10 lakh, (b) redistribution of the jurisdiction of the various DRTs, (c) modification in the existing strength of the DRTs/Debt Recovery Appellate Tribunals (DRATs), and (d) legal and institutional provisions.

Debt Securities: The term covers all tradable securities, except those classified as equity securities. Debt securities include bonds, debentures, and negotiable debt instruments etc.

Delisting of Securities: Permanent removal of securities of a listed company from a stock exchange. As a consequence of delisting, the securities of that company would no longer be traded at that stock exchange.

Delivery: Presentation of securities with transfer deeds in fulfilment of a transaction.

Delivery Notice: The written notice given by the seller of his intention to make delivery against an open short futures position on a particular date.

Dematerialisation (Demat): The concept of demat was introduced in Indian capital market in 1996 with the setting up of NSDL. Demat is the process by which the physical certificates of an investor are converted to an equivalent number of securities in electronic form and credited in the investor's account with his depository participant (DP).

When an investor decides to have his shares in electronic form, he should approach a depository participant (DP)—who is an agent of the depository—and open an account. He should then request for the dematerialisation of certificates by filling up a dematerialisation request form (DRF), which is available with the DP and submitting the same along with the physical certificates.

The investor has to ensure that before the certificates are handed over to the DP for demat, they are defaced by marking *surrendered for dematerialisation* on the face of the certificates. Before defacing the share certificate, the investor must ensure that it is available for dematerialisation. The investor must therefore check with his depository participant (DP) whether the ISIN (code number for the security in a depository system) has been activated and made available for dematerialisation by the depository. If yes, then the investor may deface the share certificate. Only those certificates can be dematerialised that are already registered in the investor's name and are in the list of securities admitted for dematerialization by National Securities Depository Limited (NSDL).

His DP will arrange to get them sent to and verified by the company, and on confirmation credit his account with an equivalent number of shares. This process is known as dematerialisation (demat). An investor can always reverse this process if he so desires and get his shares reconverted into paper format. This process is known as rematerialisation.

Benefits of Demat: These are the following:

1. Elimination of bad deliveries.
2. Elimination of all risks associated with physical certification.
3. No stamp duty.
4. Immediate transfer and registration of securities.
5. Faster settlement cycle.
6. Faster disbursement of rights, bonus etc.
7. Reduction in brokerage by many brokers for trading in dematerialised securities.
8. Reduction in handling of huge volumes of paper and postal delays.
9. Periodic status report.
10. Elimination of problems relating to change of address of investor, transmission etc.
11. Elimination of problems related to selling securities on behalf of a minor.
12. Ease in portfolio monitoring.

Demutualization: Process of transition from *mutually-owned* association to a company *owned by shareholders*. In other words, transformation of the legal structure from a mutual form to a business corporation form is referred to as demutualization.

Depository Participant (DP): An agent of the depository through which it interfaces with the investor. A DP can offer depository services only after it gets proper registration from SEBI.

Depository Receipt (DR): A negotiable security issued outside India by a depository bank, on behalf of an Indian company, which represents the local Rupee denominated equity shares of the company held as deposit by a custodian bank in India. DRs listed and traded in the US markets are known as American Depository Receipts (ADRs) and those listed and traded anywhere/elsewhere are known as Global Depository Receipts (GDRs).

Depository System: Shares are traditionally held in physical or paper form. This method has weaknesses like loss/theft of certificates, forged/fake certificates, cumbersome and time consuming procedure for transfer of shares etc. To eliminate these weaknesses, a new system called depository system has been established. A depository is a system which holds your shares in the form of electronic accounts in the same way a bank holds your money in a savings account. A depository holds securities in dematerialised form. It maintains ownership records of securities in a book entry form and also effects transfer of ownership through book entry.

Depository system provides the following advantages to an investor:

1. Shares cannot be lost, stolen or mutilated.
2. An investor never needs to doubt the genuineness of his shares i.e. whether they are forged or fake.
3. Share transactions like transfer, transmission etc. can be effected immediately.
4. Transaction costs are usually lower than on the physical segment.
5. There is no risk of bad delivery.
6. Bonus/rights shares allotted to an investor will be immediately credited to his account.
7. An investor receives the statement of accounts of his transactions/holdings periodically.

When you decide to have your shares in electronic form, you should approach a depository participant (DP) who is an agent of the depository, and open an account. You should surrender your share certificates in physical form, and your DP will arrange to get them sent to and verified by the company, and on confirmation credit your account with an equivalent number of shares. This process is known as dematerialisation (demat, for short). You can always reverse this process if you so desire and get your shares reconverted into paper format. This process is known as rematerialisation.

Share transactions (like sale or purchase and transfer/ transmission, etc.) in the electronic form can be effected in a much simpler and faster way. All you need to do is that after confirmation of sales/purchase transaction by your broker, you should approach your DP with a request to debit/credit your account for the transaction. The Depository will immediately arrange to complete the transaction by updating your account. There is no need for separate communication to the company to register the transfer.

SEBI has introduced some degree of compulsion in trading and settlement of securities in demat form while the investors have a right to hold securities in either physical or demat form, SEBI has mandated compulsory trading and settlement of securities in select securities in dematerialised form. This was initially introduced for institutional investors and was later extended to all investors.

Depreciation: A fall in value of a security or security index or a currency in terms of others or its purchasing power.

Depth of Market: The number of shares of a security that can be bought or sold at the best bid or offer price.

Deregulation: The process of removing legal or quasi legal restriction on the type of business done or on the prices charged, within a particular industry. The aim of most deregulations is to increase competition by increasing the freedom of players in the industry.

Derivative Instruments: See Credit Derivatives, *49* and Financial Derivatives, *78*.

Derivative Market: See Credit Derivatives, *49* and Financial Derivatives, *78*.

Derivatives: See Credit Derivatives, *49* and Financial Derivatives, *78*.

Development Finance Institutions (DFIs): DFIs were set up in India at various points of time starting from the late 1940s to cater to the medium to long-term financing requirements of industry as the capital market in India had not developed sufficiently. After Independence in 1947, the national government adopted the path of planned economic development and launched the First Five Year Plan in 1951. This strategy of development provided the critical inducement for establishment of DFIs at both all-India and state-levels. In order to perform their role, DFIs were extended funds of the RBI and government guaranteed bonds, which constituted major sources of their funds. Funds from these sources were not only available at concessional rates, but also on a long-term basis with their maturity period ranging from 10-15 years. On the asset side, their operations were marked by near absence of competition.

A large variety of financial institutions have come into existence over the years to perform various types of financial activities. While some of them operate at all-India level, others are state level institutions. Besides providing direct loans (including rupee loans, foreign currency loans), financial institutions also extend financial assistance by way of underwriting and direct subscription and by issuing guarantees. Recently, some DFIs have started extending short-term/working capital finance, although term-lending continues to be their primary activity.

Dirty Float: A floating security whose value is not solely determined by free market supply and demand pressures but also by interventions of the concerned authorities.

Disclosure: Full and material information given by a company that may allow an investor to take an informed investment decision.

Disclosure Norms: The central goal of securities market is to obtain a widely-dispersed ownership and trading in securities. There is conflict of interest between the management team, which controls the firm, and the shareholders, who run the firm. Many policy efforts in recent years have been devoted towards improving incentives to managers to maximise the interests of shareholders.

Improvements in disclosure are a central tool for containing the conflicts of interest between the managers and shareholders. In order to foster improvements in disclosure, SEBI set up a system named electronic data information filing and retrieval (EDIFAR) in July 2002. This system offers a mechanism through which firms would electronically file mandatory disclosures to SEBI, and these documents would be available to individuals over the internet, with a near-zero delay. It is envisaged that in the future, disclosure would take place through company websites, exchange websites, and EDIFAR.

For strengthening the process of information flow from the listed companies, several measures have been introduced: (a) while sufficient disclosures are mandatory for the companies at the stage of public issues, the listed companies are also required under the listing agreement to make disclosures on a continued basis, (b) for ensuring quick flow of information to the public, the decision pertaining to dividend, bonus and right announcements or any material event are now required to be disclosed to the public within 15 minutes of the conclusion of the board meeting in which the disclosures are taken, and (c) accounting practices have been streamlined with norms introduced for segment reporting, related to party transactions and consolidated balance sheets.

Without seeking to control the freedom of the issuers to enter the market and freely price their issues, the norms for public issues were made stringent in April 1996 to prevent fraudulent companies from accessing the market. Issuers of capital are now required to disclose information on various aspects such as track record of profitability, risk factors etc. As a result, there has been an improvement in the standards of disclosure in the offer documents for the public and rights issues and easier accessibility of information to the investors. The improvement in disclosure standards has enhanced transparency, thereby improving the level of investor protection.

Diversification: Spreading the risk by constructing a portfolio that contains many different investments whose returns are relatively uncorrelated. Thus, risk levels can be reduced without a corresponding reduction in returns.

Dividend: Payment made to shareholders, usually once or twice a year out of a company's profit after tax. Dividend payments do not distribute the entire net profit of a company, a part of which is held back as reserves for the company's expansion. Dividend is declared on the face value or par value of a share, and not on its market price.

Domestic Financial Integration: It entails horizontal linkages of various segments, reflecting portfolio diversification by savers, investors and intermediaries. Under horizontal integration, market interest rates typically revolve around a basic reference rate, which is defined as the price of a short-term low-risk financial instrument in a competitive and liquid market. Domestic markets may be closely integrated because intermediaries operate simultaneously in various market segments, for instance, commercial banks operate in both the saving (deposit) and loan markets.

Doubtful Asset: An asset would be classified as doubtful if it has remained in the substandard category for a period of 12 months. A loan classified as doubtful has all the weaknesses inherent in assets that are classified as substandard, with the added characteristic that the weaknesses make collection or liquidation in full—on the basis of currently known facts, conditions and values—highly questionable and improbable.

Dumping: In the securities market, it means the offering of large amounts of stock without regard for the effect on prices on the market. In international trade, it means selling of goods overseas below cost to get rid of a surplus or to gain a competitive edge over the foreign firms.

Ee

Earning Per Share: It means profit over a given period, reduced by preference dividend, divided by the number of shares outstanding at the end of that period.

Earning to Price Ratio: It is the ratio of the earning per share of a company to the market price of one share of that company.

Electronic Banking (e-banking): It is a generic term encompassing internet banking, telephone banking, mobile banking etc.

In other words, it is a process of delivery of banking services and products through electronic channels such as telephone, internet, cell phone etc. The concept and scope of e-banking is still evolving.

Electronic Clearing Services (ECS): ECS is a retail payment system which facilitates bulk payments that can be classified as one-to-many and receipts that are many-to-one. The two components of this system are ECS (Credit) and ECS (Debit).

ECS (Credit): It facilitates the bulk payments whereby the account of the institution remitting the payment is debited and the payments remitted to beneficiaries' accounts.

This facility is mostly used for making multiple payments, like payment of dividend to investors, payment of salaries of employees by institutions etc. For this purpose, the company or entity making the payment has to have the bank account details of the individual beneficiaries.

ECS (Debit): It facilitates the collection of payments by utility companies. In this system the account of the customers of the utility company in different banks are debited and the amounts are transferred to the account of the utility company. The company providing this facility has to receive the mandate to collect funds from its customer. On receipt of the mandate, the company advises the consumer's bank to debit the payment due from the account on the due dates.

Settlement in this system currently takes place on T+0 basis and the cycle gets completed on T+1 basis. The clearing and settlement transactions through ECS occur at the respective centres. A centralised facility is available at the RBI, Mumbai to receive the ECS (Credit) files meant for credit at the other 14 RBI centres.

Electronic Data Information Filing and Retrieval System (EDIFAR): Set up by Securities and Exchange Board of India (SEBI), in association with National Informatics Centre (NIC), EDIFAR is meant to facilitate filing of certain documents/statements by the listed companies online. This involves electronic filing of information in a standard format by the companies.

Electronic Funds Transfer (EFT) System: It utilizes computer and electronic components in order to transfer money or financial assets. EFT is information-based and intangible. EFT system was introduced in the mid-1990s. EFT facilitates transfer of funds from one bank account to another. EFT system is currently permitted to be used only for government transactions and RBI-initiated payments. This system is now progressively being replaced with National Electronic Funds Transfer (NEFT) (q.v).

Electronic Money (E-money)

In recent years, there has been a gradual switchover from the use of paper-based payments media to those based on electronics. While the basic characteristics of these new instruments are by and large similar to those of paper-based instruments, the former present a different set of challenges to policy makers. E-money is one such new product which has appeared on Indian horizon recently.

Definition and Kinds of E-money: E-money may be broadly defined as an electronic store of monetary value on a technical device used for making payments to undertakings other than the issuer without necessarily involving bank accounts in the transaction, but acting as a prepaid bearer instrument. E-money can be classified into the following two broad categories:

1. Pre-paid stored value card (also called electronic purse).
2. Pre-paid software-based product that uses computer networks such as internet (also referred to as digital cash or network money).

The stored value card scheme typically uses a microprocessor chip embedded in a plastic card while software based scheme typically uses specialised software installed in a personal computer. The stored value card could be of three types:

1. Single-purpose card.
2. Closed-system or limited-purpose card.
3. General-purpose or multi-purpose card.

The single-purpose card generally with a magnetic chip recording the amount of fund therein is designed to facilitate only one type of transaction, e.g. telephone calls, public transportation, laundry, parking facilities etc. In this case the distinguishing point is that the issuer and the service provider (acceptor) are identical for the cards. These cards are expected to substitute coins and currency notes.

Closed-system or limited-purpose card is generally used in a small number of well-identified points of sale within a well-identified location such as corporate/university campus.

Multi-purpose card can perform a variety of functions with several vendors, viz. credit card, debit card, stored value card, identification card, repository of personal medical information etc. The importance of these cards is especially underscored with respect to regulatory oversight, restrictions on issuers and their implications for monetary policy. These cards may reduce demand for current accounts in the bank for likely reduction in transaction costs, and prudent portfolio management.

It is important to distinguish here the so-called *access* products, e.g. credit card and debit card from e-money. The former typically require a telephone or a personal computer with appropriate software to access the customer account before transferring the value while under e-money, the amount of value is already embedded and it may be increased or reduced without necessarily involving a personal bank account. In a sense, e-money can be construed as an electronic form of traveller's cheques (TCs). In both cases, the user pays for the instrument upfront.

Benefits of E-money: Use and spread of e-money depends upon the incentives of issuers, merchants and consumers. For issuers, the principal motivation arises from revenues to be earned from investment of outstanding balances (i.e. float income), savings of costs from reduced handling of cash and incentive of offering fee-based service to consumers and merchants besides the larger security emanating from audit trail of transactions and improved management information system.

For merchants, the trade-off would be between reduction in cost of handling physical cash vis-à-vis cost of putting in place necessary infrastructure.

For consumers, the use of e-money would depend upon the perceived security and privacy of e-money and ease with which e-money could be used which would again depend upon willingness of merchants to accept e-money. In other words, apart from security, privacy and ease, network effects are also important for wider use of e-money.

An economy like India, where cash transactions are very high, could benefit from using e-money through cost savings from printing and minting of smaller denomination notes and coins and eliminating the cost of handling, storing, transporting and insuring currency. These should also improve operational efficiency of the financial sector as also extension of banking to the urban poor and rural communities besides facilitating E-governance initiatives of governments. However, such benefits should be weighed against the need to build up the costly infrastructure to operate nationwide cashless retail payment system.

Implications of E-money for the Central Bank: Before analysing the likely implications, it is instructive to note that e-money can be issued in three alternate ways. Each of these three ways may have different implications for conduct of monetary policy.

1. E-money can be issued in exchange of cash (i.e. 100 percent backing of central bank money). Under that circumstance, there may be only marginal change in total money supply in the economy provided there is no significant change in velocity of circulation of money.
2. E-money can also be issued on credit against interest payment.
3. E-money could also be issued as a separate form of currency independent of central bank money by entities other than the central bank. In that case, e-money would compete against the central bank money as a medium of exchange. However, such a scenario in which public gets e-money from an entity in exchange for something other than the central bank money seems remote now.

Currency notes and coins generally form an overwhelming part of the balance sheet of any central bank. If e-money is extensively used and in the process, replaces substantially central bank's money, central bank's balance sheet would *shrink* while that of the issuing authority of e-money would *expand* in relative terms.

With large scale use of e-money, it is apprehended that central bank's balance sheet may shrink to such an extent relative to that of the banking sector that it may be unable to perform its liquidity absorption function [in effect, open market operations (OMO)] on account of non-availability of adequate volume of assets. Under that circumstance, extensive e-monetisation in the economy could jeopardise the conduct of monetary policy of the central bank. It may, however, be noted that the central bank would not have any problem in liquidity injection because central bank money is still the only legal tender in the economy.

Apart from constraining its liquidity management function, relative shrinkage in balance sheet may also have implications regarding loss of *seigniorage* revenue for the central bank. This is because currency notes and coins are the interest-free liability of the central bank towards public (i.e. public have in effect lent to the central bank such amount free of interest) which are then used by the central bank to purchase interest bearing assets. Thus, interest earned on these assets constitutes its seigniorage revenue. Therefore, if the central bank's operating costs are high which are more likely in an environment where central bank is required to intervene more, it may even incur losses on account of seigniorage revenue foregone. This may also have adverse implications for governments with chronic budget deficits as they would be deprived of the transfer of surplus to its treasury from the profitable central bank.

A distinguishing characteristic of e-money is that unlike innovations in other retail payments media—which facilitate more efficient access to traditional form of central bank money—e-money could have the potential to become an independent medium of exchange. In that eventuality, two extreme views are being offered. On the one hand, one group perceives that in a highly technologically-advanced networked world, private entities may not require central bank money for settlement and, therefore, there may not be any central bank in future. Some of them also question whether private money is more efficient than central bank money from social welfare viewpoint and if so under what circumstance private money can replace central bank money altogether. On the other hand, there is another group of academicians and practitioners who strongly believe that central banks would continue to be as effective as ever though they may be required to respond differently in the changed environment.

E-Money in India: In India, where cash transactions are high in number, the use of e-money can be beneficial in terms of reduced miscellaneous costs, viz. cost of printing and minting of smaller denomination notes and coins and transportation and storage costs. However, certain additional costs for setting up of network infrastructure to operate nationwide are also associated with it. The RBI has been partnering a multi-application smart card project, under the aegis of the Ministry of Communications and Information Technology, Government of India, to run a pilot project on the use of multi-application smart cards in the country. Various issues relating to technology, security, regulatory and supervisory concerns and legal implications have been examined to make the use of smart cards a viable proposition after the conclusion of the pilot project. The project is aimed at combining applications relating to banking, insurance, postal services, identification, etc in a single card.

The Reserve Bank of India had constituted a Working Group on Electronic Money (Chairman: Zaire J. Camas) in January 2002 which submitted its Report in July 2002. The Group identified certain areas of concern from the point of view of the central bank in the context of more widespread use of e-money. Some of the suggestions made by the Group included: (a) multi-purpose e-money to be issued only by authorised banks on a credit basis which should be strictly regulated and closely monitored, (b) redeemability should be ensured in order to preserve the unit of account function of money as well as to control money supply in the economy, and (c) reporting of e-money statistics should be ensured for the purposes of monetary policy and protection against criminal abuse such as money laundering.

E-money: See Electronic Money, *69*.

Employee Stock Option: It means the option given to the whole-time directors, officers or employees of a company which gives such directors, officers or employees, the benefit or right to purchase or subscribe at a future date, the securities offered by the company at a pre-determined price.

Employee Stock Purchase Scheme (ESPS): It means a scheme under which the company offers shares to employees as part of a public issue or otherwise.

Entry Fee: Fee paid by an investor when purchasing units in a trust or managed fund. The fee is included in the price that new investors pay.

Equity: The ownership interest in a company of holders of its common and preferred stock.

Equity Capital: It comprises: (a) equity in branches, (b) all shares in subsidiaries and associates (except non-participating, preferred shares that are treated as debt securities and included under direct investment, other capital), and (c) other capital contributions.

Equity Premium: The difference between the expected return from holding stock and from holding riskless bonds.

Escheat: It refers to reversion of real or personal property to the State when: (a) a person dies without leaving a will and has no heirs, or (b) when the property (such as a bank account) has been inactive for a certain period of time.

Escrow: A financial instrument held by a third party on behalf of the other two parties in a transaction. The funds are held by the escrow service until it receives the appropriate written or oral instructions—or until obligations have been fulfilled. Securities, funds, and other assets can be held in escrow.

Ex: Means *without*. A price so quoted excludes recently declared dividends (xd), rights (xr) or bonus shares (xb).

Exchange: Regulated market place where capital market products are bought and sold through intermediaries.

Exchange Rate: Exchange rate is the rate at which the currency of one country is converted into another currency. For example, ₹ 60 = 1 US$ is Indian rupee exchange rate for one US dollar. Various types of exchange rate regimes are as follows:

Nominal Exchange Rate: It is the official parity for transactions as settled by a country's monetary authority.

Effective Exchange Rate: Apart from the nominal exchange rate, it includes all surcharges, tariffs, rebates and incentives on exports.

Price Level Deflated Exchange Rate (PLD-ER): Under it, the nominal exchange rate is deflated by the price index in relation to some base period.

Purchasing Power Parity Adjusted Exchange Rate (PPPA-ER): It means the exchange rate (nominal or effective) is multiplied by the ratio of the foreign price level to domestic price level.

Real Effective Exchange Rate: In this case, the exchange rate is adjusted for inflation differentials between the country whose exchange rate is being measured and the country against which the exchange rate is calculated.

Forward and Spot Exchange Rates: Forward rate is the agreed rate of exchange at which a currency can be bought or sold today for delivery at some future date. Spot transactions are settled in two working days time. Forward exchange cover is a type of insurance that protects against movements in exchange rates and risks arising therefrom. As such, an exchange rate quoted for a forward date usually involves a premium or discount as compared with the spot rate.

Two-tier Exchange Rate: It means one exchange rate for commercial transactions and a separate exchange rate for financial transactions on current account.

Exchange Rate Risk: The risk that adverse movements in exchange rates lead to capital losses in assets or revaluation of liabilities.

Exchange Traded Funds (ETFs): An exchange-traded fund is an investment fund that is traded on a stock exchange, just like stocks. An ETF holds assets such as stocks, commodities or bonds and trades in value, around its net asset value (NAV) over the course of the trading day. Most ETFs track an index such as a stock index or a bond index. ETFs are attractive investments because of their low costs, diversified holdings, tax efficiency and stock-like features. ETFs are the most popular type of exchange-traded products in the US and Europe.

ETFs are simple and easy to understand. Most ETFs also have an intrinsically lower risk due to their diversified portfolio. This diversification coupled with low expenses allows the smallest of the investors to reap the benefits of market based returns. Retail investors can use ETF's as an easy entry vehicle into the capital markets. Equity investments are most likely to give you attractive long term growth. And, this growth is reflected in market indices, like the NSE Nifty.

Ex-Dividend Date: The date on or after which the buyer of a security is not entitled to the dividend already declared.

Exit Fees: Fees charged by mortgage trusts/mutual funds on a sliding scale as penalty for early withdrawal.

Ff

Face Value: The value that appears on the face of the scrip, same as nominal or par value of share/debentures.

Financial Derivatives: In recent years, complex financial products such as asset-backed securities, derivatives, credit-default swaps (CDSs) and collateralised debt obligations (CDOs) have proliferated in developed countries. These products have become highly popular with banks and financial institutions as they allow them to hedge their risks and manage their regulatory and economic capital more efficiently.

The emergence of the market for derivative products, most notably forwards, futures and options, can be traced back to the willingness of risk-averse economic agents to guard themselves against uncertainties arising out of fluctuations in asset prices. By their very nature, the financial markets are marked by a very high degree of volatility. Through the use of derivative products, it is possible to partially or fully transfer price risks by locking-in asset prices. As instruments of risk management, derivatives generally do not influence the fluctuations in the underlying asset prices. However, by locking-in asset prices, derivative products minimize the impact of fluctuations in asset prices on the profitability and cash flow situation of risk-averse investors.

Derivative products initially emerged as hedging devices against fluctuations in commodity prices and commodity-linked derivatives remained the sole form of such products for a long time. The financial derivatives came into spotlight in post-1970 period due to growing instability in the financial markets. However, since their emergence, financial derivatives have become very popular. In recent years, the market for financial derivatives has grown tremendously both in terms of variety of instruments available, their complexity and also turnover.

In India also financial products such as mortgage-backed securities (MBS) and asset-backed securities (ABS) are in existence. Besides the securitised products, the Indian forex and rupee derivative markets have also developed significantly over the years.

In respect of forex derivatives involving rupee, residents have access to foreign exchange forward contracts, foreign currency-rupee swap instruments and currency options—both cross currency and foreign currency-rupee. As stated in the Annual Policy Statement for the year 2008-09, the Reserve Bank of India (RBI) announced the introduction of currency futures in the eligible exchanges for which the broad framework was announced in August 2008. In future, some more innovative and complex products might emerge. These products may pose several regulatory and supervisory challenges.

Meaning of Derivatives: Derivative in mathematics means a variable derived from another variable. The term *derivative* indicates that it has no independent value, i.e. its value is entirely *derived* from the value of the underlying asset. The underlying asset can be security, commodity, bullion, currency, live stock or anything else. In other words, derivative means a forward, future, option or any other hybrid contract of pre-determined fixed duration, linked for the purpose of contract fulfilment to the value of a specified real or financial asset of an index of securities. Similarly, in the financial sense, a derivative is a financial product, which has been derived from a market for another product. Without the underlying product, derivatives do not have any independent existence in the market.

Derivative instruments are defined by the Indian Securities Contracts (Regulation) Act, 1956 to include: (i) a security derived from a debt instrument, share, secured/unsecured loan, risk instrument or contract for differences, or any other form of security, and (ii) a contract that derives its value from the prices/index of prices of underlying securities.

In other words, derivatives are financial instruments/contracts whose value depends upon the value of an underlying. Since their value is essentially derived out of an underlying, they are financial abstractions whose value is derived mathematically from the changes in the value of the underlying.

The International Monetary Fund (IMF) defines derivatives as "financial instruments that are linked to a specific financial instrument or indicator or commodity and through which specific financial risks can be traded in financial markets in their own right. The value of a financial derivative derives from the price of an underlying item, such as an asset or index. Unlike debt securities, no principal is advanced to be repaid and no investment income accrues".

Derivatives have come into being because of the existence of risks in business. Thus, derivatives are means of managing risks. The parties managing risks in the market are known as *hedgers*. Some people/organizations are in the business of taking risks to earn profits. Such entities represent the *speculators*. The third players in the market, known as the *arbitragers,* take advantage of the market mistakes.

In recent years, derivatives have become increasingly important in the field of finance. While futures and options are now actively traded on many exchanges, forward contracts are popular on the over-the-counter (OTC) market.

Reasons for the Popularity of Derivatives: Financial derivatives have become popular due to the following reasons:

1. Increased volatility in asset prices in financial markets.
2. Increased integration of national financial markets with the international markets.
3. Marked improvement in communication facilities and sharp decline in their costs.
4. Development of more sophisticated risk management tools, providing economic agents a wider choice of risk management strategies.
5. Innovations in the derivatives markets, which optimally combine the risks and returns over a large number of financial assets, leading to higher returns, reduced risk as well as transaction costs as compared to individual financial assets.

In the class of equity derivatives, futures and options on stock indices have gained more popularity than on individual stocks, especially among institutional investors, who are major users of index-linked derivatives. Even small investors find these useful due to high correlation of the popular indices with various portfolios and ease of use. The lower costs associated with index derivatives vis-à-vis derivative products based on individual securities is another reason for their growing use.

Variants (or Types) of Derivative Contracts: Derivative contracts have several variants. The most common variants are forwards, futures, options and swaps.

Forwards/Forward Contracts: A forward contract is a customised contract between two entities, where settlement takes place on a specific date in the future at today's pre-agreed price. A forward contract is an agreement to buy or sell an asset on a specified date for specified price. One of the parties to the contract assumes a long position and agrees to buy the underlying asset on a certain specified future date, for a certain specified price. The other party assumes a short position and agrees to sell the asset on the same date for the same price. Other contract details like delivery date, price and quantity are negotiated bilaterally by the parties to the contract. See also full entry on Forwards/Forward Contracts.

Futures/Future Contracts: Future contracts are special types of forward contracts in the sense that the former are standardised exchange-traded contracts. Future contract markets are designed to solve the problems that exist in forward markets. A future contract is an agreement between two parties to buy or sell an asset at a certain time in future, at a certain price. However, unlike forward contracts, future contracts are standardized and stock exchange-traded. To facilitate liquidity in the future contracts, the exchange specifies certain standard features for the contract. It is a standardized contract with a standard underlying instrument, a standard quantity and quality of the underlying instrument that can be delivered, and a standard timing of such settlement. See also full entry on Futures/Future Contracts.

Options: Options are fundamentally different from forward and future contracts. An option gives the holder of the option the right to do something. The holder does not have to necessarily exercise this right. In contrast, in a forward or future contract, the two parties commit themselves to doing something. Whereas it costs nothing (except margin requirements) to enter into a future contract, the purchase of an option requires an up front payment.

Options are of two types: calls options and put options. Call options give the buyer the right but not the obligation to buy a given quantity of the underlying asset, at a given price on or before a given future date. Put options give the buyer the right, but not the obligation to sell a given quantity of the underlying asset at a given price on or before a given date. See also full entry on Options.

Swaps: Swaps are private agreements between two parties to exchange cash flows in the future according to a pre-arranged formula. They can be regarded as portfolios of forward contracts. Following are the two commonly used swaps:

- **Interest Rate Swaps:** These entail swapping of only the interest-related cash flows between the parties in the same currency.
- **Currency Swaps:** These entail swapping of both principal and interest between the parties, with the cash flows in one direction being in a different currency than those in the opposite direction.

Swaptions: Swaptions are options to buy or sell a swap that will become operative at the expiry of the options. Thus, swaption is an option on a forward swap. Rather than have call options and put options, the swaptions market has receiver swaptions and payer swaptions.

Participants in the Derivatives Market: The following three broad categories of participants, viz. hedgers, speculators, and arbitrageurs trade in the derivatives market.

Hedgers: Hedgers face risk associated with the price of an asset. They use future or option markets to reduce or eliminate this risk. In other words, hedgers are those who wish to protect their existing exposures and essentially are safety-driven.

Speculators: They bet on future movements in the price of an asset. Future and option contracts can give them an extra leverage; that is, they can increase both the potential gains and potential losses in a speculative venture. Speculators are willing risk takers who are expectation-driven.

Arbitrageurs: They are in business to take advantage of a discrepancy between prices in two different markets. If, for example, they see the futures price of an asset getting out of line with the cash price, they will take offsetting positions in the two markets to lock-in a profit. Arbitragers are traders and market-makers who deal in buying and selling derivatives contracts hoping to profit from price-differentials between different markets. A market maker is one who provides two-way quotes for a given product and thereby runs a position in that product.

Economic Role of Derivatives: Derivative markets perform three essential economic functions:

1. Risk management.
2. Price discovery.
3. Transactional efficiency.

The first function refers to the ability of traders to offset financial risks through derivatives. The principal benefit of the derivatives market is that it provides the opportunity for risk management through hedging. Derivatives are innovations in risk management not in risk itself.

The second refers to the better allocation of resources in an economy that is created by the wide availability of an equilibrium price which serves as a measure of value.

The third function alludes to increased efficiency of transacting through derivatives. Derivative markets reduce the costs of trading and raising capital, thereby enhancing their risk management and price discovery functions.

Derivatives have played a major role in the development of financial markets and their integration across several economies, especially in developed countries. Derivatives serve to achieve a more complete financial system because previously fixed combinations of the risk properties of loans and financial assets can be bundled and unbundled into new synthetic assets. For instance, structured products or synthetic derivatives could be created by adding elementary assets or underlying assets such as bonds, equities and borrowing and lending instruments with a combination of derivative products such as put and call options. Repackaging risk properties in this way can provide a more perfect match between an investor's risk preferences and the effective risk of the portfolio or cash-flow. Derivatives allow individual risk elements of an asset to be priced and traded individually, thus ensuring an efficient price system in the asset markets.

The economic functions performed by derivatives market can be summarised as under:

1. Derivatives market helps to increase savings and investment in the long-run. Transfer of risk enables market participants to expand their volume of activity.
2. Derivatives trading acts as a catalyst for new entrepreneurial activity. Derivatives have a history of attracting many bright, creative, well educated people with an entrepreneurial attitude.
3. Prices in an organized derivatives market reflect the perception of the market participants about the future and lead the prices of underlying to the perceived future level.
4. Prices of derivatives converge with the prices of the underlying at the expiration of the derivatives contract. In fact, derivatives help in the discovery of the future as well as current prices.
5. Derivatives market helps to transfer risks from those who have them but may not like them to those who have an appetite for them.
6. Derivatives, due to their inherent nature are linked to the underlying cash markets. With the introduction of derivatives, the underlying market witnesses higher trading volumes because of participation by more players who would not otherwise participate for lack of an arrangement to transfer risk.
7. Speculative trades shift to a more controlled environment of

derivatives market. In the absence of an organized derivatives market, speculators trade in the underlying cash markets. Margining, monitoring and surveillance of the activities of various participants become extremely difficult in these kinds of mixed markets.

Derivative Instruments in India: India has introduced different equity derivatives in a phased manner. This phased approach was adopted in India with index futures being introduced in June 2000, index options in June 2001 and individual stock options in July 2001.

Derivatives trading commenced in India in June 2000 after SEBI granted the final approval to this effect in May 2000. SEBI permitted the derivatives segments of two stock exchanges NSE and BSE, and their clearing house/corporation to commence trading and settlement in approved derivative contracts. To begin with, SEBI approved trading in index future contracts based on S&P CNX Nifty and BSE-30 (Sensex) index. This was followed by approval for trading in options which commenced in June 2001 and the trading in options on individual securities commenced in July 2001. Future contracts on individual stocks were launched in November 2001. Trading and settlement in derivative contracts is done in accordance with the rules, byelaws, and regulations of the respective exchanges and their clearing house/corporation duly approved by SEBI and notified in the official gazette.

The derivatives market got a shot in the arm with the Government deciding to treat income from derivatives trading as a non-speculative income.

The decision to treat income from derivative trading as a non-speculative income will contribute to an increase in trading volume in the derivative market since it provides for setting off of derivative income/loss against normal income/loss.

FIIs are permitted to submit appropriate collateral, in cash or otherwise when trading in domestic derivatives. According to market players, this will bring about flexibility and encourage FIIs to take greater exposure through the derivative contracts.

Local players already had the flexibility of submitting collaterals, such as bank guarantee or shares or deposit receipt, in place of cash or along with cash, for meeting their margin obligations. See also Credit Derivatives.

Financial Intermediaries: Financial intermediaries are an integral part of a modern industrial economy. They are institutions which act as middlemen between the lenders and the borrowers. They specialise in the purchase and sale of financial assets. More specifically, they buy primary securities and sell secondary securities. Financial intermediaries are classified into two main categories: (a) banks, and (b) non-banking financial institutions like Unit Trust of India (q.v.).

Financial intermediaries are beneficial both to lenders and borrowers. Lenders stand to gain because they can invest their funds at low risk and greater liquidity with financial institutions. The main advantage to borrowers is availability of adequate credit at reasonable rate of interest. How are financial intermediaries able to benefit both lenders and borrowers and also to make profit for themselves in the process? The secret of their economic success lies in the economies of scale in asset management. They diversify their asset holdings in such a manner as to strike an optimum balance between security and profitability. For this purpose, the financial institutions employ professional managers and financial analysts who evaluate investment opportunities and take appropriate decisions. Because of the large volume of business, the establishment cost per unit of transaction is lower as compared to that of an individual investor.

Financial Market: It is a market in which financial assets of various kinds like shares, debentures and bills are dealt with. A financial market consists of: (a) money market which deals in short-term credit, and (b) capital market which provides medium-term and long-term credit.

In a developing country like India money market is sub-divided into: (a) organised market, and (b) unorganised market. Commercial banks, co-operative banks and non-banking financial institutions comprise the organised sector of the money market.

This market operates under the control, guidance and supervision of the central bank. The unorganised money market predominates in rural areas and is composed of indigenous bankers and moneylenders. It is generally free from the monetary and credit controls of the central bank. It operates without a set of well-defined rules and regulations and is, therefore, exploitative in its dealings. The malpractices of moneylenders are well-known.

Like money market, the capital market is also divided into two sectors: (a) organised market comprising of development banks, share market and mutual funds, and (b) unorganised market consisting of hire purchase companies, chit funds, finance companies etc. The unorganised sector of the capital market has limited importance.

Financial Repression: It is a term meaning excessive government controls on financial system of a country. It includes: (a) high required reserve ratios, (b) subsidised or directed credit programmes, (c) credit rationing, (d) ceilings on deposit, and (e) fixing maximum interest rates on loans.

Financial System: It refers to the whole gamut of institutional arrangements which help to mobilise financial surpluses of an economy and transfer them to areas of financial deficit. Financial system of a country rests on three pillars: (a) financial institutions or financial intermediaries, (b) financial markets and (c) financial assets. Financial system is the linchpin of a modern industrial economy. It promotes savings by providing a wide variety of financial assets to the general public. Savings collected from the household sector are pooled together and allocated to various sectors of the economy for raising production level. If the allocation of credit is socially equitable, it will help in reducing interregional inequalities.

Financial Year: It is the year of account for financial purposes, often not coinciding with the calendar year. For example, in India the financial year (or fiscal year) runs from April 1 to March 31 of the following year. In US, the fiscal year runs from July 1 to June 30.

Firewall: A barrier designed to prevent losses or risks taken in one part of a financial institution from weakening other parts of institution.

Firm Allotment: Allotment on a firm basis in public issues by an issuing company made to Indian and multilateral development financial institutions, Indian mutual funds, foreign institutional investors including non-resident Indians and overseas corporate bodies and permanent/regular employees of the issuer company.

Fixed Asset: An item of value used in current operation that would normally be of use for more than one year.

Fixed Liability: An obligation of a company payable more than a year hence.

Floor: Trading hall of the stock exchange where transactions in securities take place. The trading ring where members and their assistants assemble with their order books for executing the order of their constituents.

Floor Price: The minimum offer price below which bids cannot be entered. The issuer company in consultation with the lead book runner fixes the floor price.

Foreign Direct Investment (FDI): Investment in a country by individuals and organisations from other countries is an important aspect of international finance. This flow of international finance may take the form of direct investment (creation of productive facilities) or portfolio investment (acquisition of securities).

FDI is the outcome of the mutual interests of multinational firms and host countries. According to the International Monetary Fund (IMF), FDI is defined as "investment that is made to acquire a lasting interest in an enterprise operating in an economy other than that of the investor. The investor's purpose being to have an effective voice in the management of the enterprise". The essence of FDI is the transmission to the host country of a package of capital, managerial, skill and technical knowledge. FDI is generally a form of long-term international capital movement, made for the purpose of productive activity and accompanied by the intention of managerial control or participation in the management of a foreign firm.

In India, FDI means investment by non-resident entity/person resident outside India in the capital of an Indian company under Schedule 1 of Foreign Exchange Management (Transfer or Issue of Security by a Person Resident Outside India) Regulations, 2000.

FDI is usually contrasted with Portfolio Investment (q.v) which does not seek management control, but is motivated by profit. Portfolio investment occurs when individual investors invest, mostly through stockbrokers, in stocks of foreign companies in foreign land in search of profit opportunities.

However, the distinction between FDI and portfolio investment is not watertight because sometimes FDI policy and portfolio investments are intertwined.

Foreign Exchange Management Act (FEMA), 1999: Realising that Foreign Exchange Regulation Act (FERA), 1973 was not in tune with the economic reforms initiated since 1991, the Government replaced it with a new legislation, viz. Foreign Exchange Management Act (FEMA), 1999 which came into effect from June 1, 2000. FERA, 1973 remained a nightmare for 27 years for the Indian corporate world. The objective of the new legislation as stated in the preamble to the Act is *to facilitate external trade and payments and promote the orderly development and maintenance of the foreign exchange market in India*—a shift in the approach from *conservation of foreign exchange resources of the country and the proper utilisation thereof* under the FERA, 1973.

Under FEMA, foreign exchange law violators are treated as civil offenders rather than as criminals as was the case under

FERA, 1973. Contravention of the provisions of FEMA invites monetary penalties. Moreover, FEMA provides for a number of appellate authorities who can be approached by the aggrieved party against whom penalties have been levied. A qualitative change has been brought about in the legal framework by FEMA. The objectives of regulation have been redefined as facilitating trade and payments as well as orderly development and maintenance of foreign exchange market in India. The legal framework envisages both the developmental dimension and orderliness or stability. The legislation provides power to the government to re-impose controls if public interest warrants it.

The shift in the policy approach entailed significant implications for the operations of the RBI. Under the new system, all current account payments except those notified by the government are eligible for appropriate foreign currency in respect of genuine transactions from the authorised dealers without any restrictions. The surrender requirements in respect of exports of goods and services continue to operate. The RBI would, however, have the necessary regulatory jurisdiction over capital account transactions.

Distinguishing Features of FEMA, 1999: The reforms in industrial and trade policies initiated in the early 1990s, consistent with the changing international economic and trade relations, gave rise to the need for a more conducive climate for increased inflow of foreign investment and capital to accelerate the pace of industrial growth and export promotion. The FEMA diluted the rigorous enforcement provisions of FERA, 1973. Under FEMA: (a) the prosecution has to prove the guilt of the accused person, (b) only monetary penalty is provided for contraventions, (c) contravention of FEMA provisions are dealt with under civil procedures, for which separate administrative mechanisms in the form of Compounding Rules, Adjudicating Authority, Special Director (Appeals) and Appellate Tribunal have been established, and (d) for each process of law a timeframe has been provided in the Act.

The concept of compounding is an important feature of FEMA. Under FERA, 1973, all violations were subject to separate investigation and adjudication of the Directorate of Enforcement. The FEMA provides an opportunity of seeking compounding of contraventions, in terms of which a contravener has a *suo moto* opportunity of making an application to the compounding authority seeking the contravention to be compounded. The compounding authority is required to dispose of the application within 180 days.

The Government of India, in one of the recent Notifications, has designated the RBI as the compounding authority for all contraventions under the FEMA, except for those involving *hawala* transactions for which the Directorate of Enforcement would be the compounding authority. The new procedure provides quick and hassle-free disposal of the cases involving contravention(s) of FEMA.

Foreign Institutional Investor (FII): An institution established or incorporated outside India which proposes to make investment in India in securities; provided that a domestic asset management company or domestic portfolio manager who manages funds raised or collected or brought from outside India for investment in India on behalf of a sub-account, shall be deemed to be a foreign institutional investor.

Foreign Investment Implementation Authority (FIIA): FIIA was established in the Department of Industrial Policy and Promotion, Ministry of Commerce and Industry in 1999 to assist the foreign investors in getting necessary approvals and thereby facilitating quick translation of FDI approvals into implementation. The FIIA also helps foreign investors in sorting out operational problems and meeting with various government agencies to find solution to problems of the investors.

Foreign Investment Promotion Board (FIPB): It is a specially empowered board in India, chaired by Secretary, Department of Economic Affairs, Ministry of Finance, which acts as the approving authority for foreign investment not falling under the automatic approval route. It also acts as a facilitator/single-window clearance agency for large foreign investment proposals.

Foreign Investment Promotion Council (FIPC): Apart from making the policy framework investor-friendly and transparent, promotional measures are also taken to attract FDI into the country. Government has constituted FIPC in the Ministry of Commerce and Industry. This comprises professionals from industry and commerce. It has been set up to have a more target-oriented approach toward FDI promotion. The basic function of FIPC is to identify specific sectors/projects within the country that require FDI and target specific regions/countries of the world for its mobilisation.

Foreign Venture Capital Investor (FVCI): An investor—incorporated and established outside India—which is registered under the Securities and Exchange Board of India (Foreign Venture Capital Investor) Regulations, 2000 [SEBI(FVCI) Regulations] and proposes to make investment in accordance with these Regulations.

Forward Markets Commission (FMC): FMC is the chief regulator of forwards and futures markets in India. It is headquartered in Mumbai and unusually for a financial regulatory agency is overseen by the Ministry of Consumer Affairs, Food and Public Distribution, Government of India.

Established in 1953 under the provisions of the Forward Contracts (Regulation) Act, 1952, it consists of 2 to 4 members, all appointed by the Government of India. Currently, the Commission allows commodity trading in 22 exchanges in India, of which 3 are national.

FMC falls under the Ministry of Consumer Affairs, Food and Public Distribution and not the Ministry of Finance as in most countries. This is because futures, traded in India, are traditionally on food commodities.

Just at the time the FMC was established, the Government felt that derivative markets increased speculation which led to increased costs and price instabilities. Therefore, options and futures trading was prohibited altogether in 1953.

The industry was pushed underground and the prohibition meant that development and expansion came to a halt. As futures and options markets began to develop in the rest of the world, Indian derivatives markets were left behind. The apprehensions about the role of speculation, particularly in the conditions of scarcity, prompted the Government to continue the prohibition well into the 1980s.

This left the country with a large number of small and isolated regional futures markets. The futures markets are dispersed and fragmented, with separate trading communities in different regions with little contact with one another. The exchanges generally have yet to embrace modern technology or modern business practices.

Next to the officially approved exchanges, there are many *havala* markets. Most of these unofficial commodity exchanges have operated for many decades. Some unofficial markets trade 20 to 30 times the volume of the *official* futures exchanges. They offer not only futures, but also option contracts. Transaction costs are low, and they attract many speculators and the smaller hedgers. Absence of regulation and proper clearing arrangements, however, mean that these markets are mostly *regulated* by the reputation of the main players.

The responsibilities and functions of Forward Markets Commission (FMC) are as follows:

1. To advise the Central Government in respect of the recognition or the withdrawal of recognition from any association or in respect of any other matter arising out of the administration of the Forward Contracts (Regulation) Act, 1952.
2. To keep forward markets under observation and to take such action in relation to them, as it may consider necessary, in exercise of the powers assigned to it by or under the Act.
3. To collect and, whenever the Commission thinks it necessary,

publish information regarding the trading conditions in respect of goods to which any of the provisions of the Act is made applicable, including information regarding supply, demand and prices, and to submit to the Central Government, periodical reports on the working of forward markets relating to such goods.

4. To make recommendations generally with a view to improving the organization and working of forward markets.
5. To undertake the inspection of the accounts and other documents of any recognized association or registered association or any member of such association whenever it considers it necessary.

It allows futures trading in 23 fibres and manufacturers, 15 spices, 44 edible oils, 6 pulses, 4 energy products, single vegetable, 20 metal futures, 33 others futures.

Forwards/Forward Contracts: A forward contract is a particularly simple derivative. A deal for the purchase or sale of a commodity, security or other asset can be in the spot or forward markets. A spot or cash market is the most commonly used for trading. A majority of day to day transaction are in the cash market, where we pay cash and get the delivery of the goods. In addition to a cash purchase, another way to acquire or sell assets is by entering into a forward contract. In a forward contract, the buyer agrees to pay cash at a later date when the seller delivers the goods.

A forward contract is an agreement to buy or sell an asset on a specified date for a specified price. One of the parties to the contract assumes a long position and agrees to buy the underlying asset on a certain specified future date for a certain specified price. The other party assumes a short position and agrees to sell the asset on the same date for the same price. Other contract details like delivery date, price and quantity are negotiated bilaterally by the parties to the contract. The forward contracts are normally traded outside the exchanges.

Salient Features of Forward Contracts: These are as under:

1. They are bilateral contracts and hence exposed to counterparty risk.
2. Each contract is custom designed, and hence is unique in terms of contract size, expiration date and the asset type and quality.
3. Contract price is generally not available in public domain.
4. On the expiration date, the contract has to be settled by delivery of the asset.
5. If the party wishes to reverse the contract, it has to compulsorily go to the same counterparty, which often results in high prices being charged.

Usually no money changes hands when forward contracts are entered into, but sometimes one or both the parties to a contract may like to ask for some initial, good-faith deposits to insure that the contract is honoured by the other party.

A forward contract is settled at maturity. The holder of the short position delivers the asset to the holder price. A forward contract is worth zero when it is first entered into. Later it can have position or negative value, depending on movements in the price of the asset.

However, forward contracts in certain markets have become much standardised, as in the case of foreign exchange, thereby reducing transaction costs and increasing transaction volumes. This process of standardisation reaches its limit in the organised futures market.

Advantages of Forwards: Forward contracts are very useful in hedging and speculation. A typical hedging application would be that of an exporter who expects to receive payment in dollars 3 months later. He is exposed to the risk of exchange rate fluctuations. By using the currency forward market to sell dollars forward, he can lock-on to a rate today and reduce his uncertainty. Similarly, an importer who is required to make a payment in dollars 2 months hence can reduce his exposure to exchange rate fluctuations by buying dollars forward.

In a forward contract the price at which the underlying commodity or assets will be traded, is decided at the time of entering into the contract. The essential idea of entering into the forward contract is to peg the price and thereby avoid the price risk. Thus by entering in the forward contract, one is assured of the price at which one can buy/sell goods or other assets. Manufacturers using a certain raw material whose price is subject to variation, can avoid the risk of price moving adversely by entering into a forward contract and plan their operations better. Similarly, by entering into a forward contract, a farmer can ensure the price he can get for his crops and not worry about what price would prevail at the time of maturity of the contract. Of course, at the time of maturity of contract, if the market price of the commodity is greater than the price agreed, then the buyer stands to gain. The opposite would hold when the market price is lower than the agreed price.

If a speculator has information or analysis, which forecasts an upturn in a price, then he can go long on the forward market instead of the cash market. The speculator would go long on the forward, wait for the price to rise, and then take a reversing transaction to book profits. Speculators may well be required to deposit a margin upfront. However, this is generally a relatively small proportion of the value of the assets underlying the forward contract. The use of forward markets supplies leverage to the speculator.

Problems of Forward Contracts: A forward contract is evidently a good mean of avoiding price risk, but it entails elements of risk in that a party to the contract may not honour its part of the obligation. Thus, each party is at risk of default. There is another problem. Once a position of buyer and seller takes in a forward contract, an investor cannot retreat except through mutual consent with the party or by entering into an identical contract and taking a position that is the reverse of earlier position. Alternatives are by no means easy. With forward contract entered on a one-to-one basis and with no standardization, the forward contract has virtually no liquidity. This problem of credit risk and no liquidity associated with forward contracts led to the emergence of future contracts. Future contracts are the refined version of forward contracts.

Forward markets world-wide are afflicted by several problems:

1. Lack of centralisation of trading.
2. Illiquidity.
3. Counterparty risk.

In the first two of these, the basic problem is that of too much flexibility and generality. The forward market is like a real estate market in that any two consenting adults can form contracts against each other. This often makes them design terms of the deal which are very convenient in that specific situation, but makes the contract non-tradable. Counterparty risk arises from the possibility of default by any one party to the transaction. When one of the two sides to the transaction declares bankruptcy, the other suffers. Even when forward markets trade standardised contracts, and hence avoid the problem of illiquidity, still the counterparty risk remains a very serious issue.

Fraud: Frauds have been classified as under, based mainly on the provisions of the Indian Penal Code:

1. Misappropriation and criminal breach of trust.
2. Fraudulent encashment through forged instruments, manipulation of books of account or through fictitious accounts and conversion of property.
3. Unauthorised credit facilities extended for reward or for illegal gratification.
4. Negligence and cash shortages.
5. Cheating and forgery.
6. Irregularities in foreign exchange transactions.
7. Any other type of fraud not coming under the specific heads as above.

Free Cash Flow: Calculated by adding depreciation to net income, and subtracting capital expenditures. Free cash flow represents the cash that is available to a company to spend after financing a capital project.

Free Pricing: Raising of capital from the securities market before 1992 was regulated under the Capital Issues (Control) Act, 1947. Firms were required to obtain approval from the Controller of Capital Issues (CCI) for raising resources in the market. New companies were allowed to issue shares only at par. Only the existing companies with substantial reserves could issue shares at a premium, which was based on some prescribed formula. In 1992, the Capital Issues (Control) Act, 1947 was repealed and with this ended all controls related to raising of resources from the market. Since then the issuers of securities can raise capital from the market without requiring any consent from any authority, either for making the issue or for pricing it. Restrictions on rights and bonus issues have also been removed. New as well as established companies are now able to price their issues according to their assessment of market conditions.

However, issuers of capital are required to meet the guidelines of SEBI on disclosure and investor protection. Companies issuing capital are required to make sufficient disclosures, including justification of the issue price and also material disclosure about the risk factors in their offer prospectus. These guidelines have served as an important measure for protecting the interest of investors and promoting the development of primary market along sound lines.

It may be recalled that in the early 1990s, the liberalisation of the industrial sector and free pricing of capital issues led to an increased number of companies tapping the primary capital market to mobilise resources. Several corporates charged a high premium not justified by their fundamentals.

Also, several companies vanished after raising resources from the capital market. SEBI, therefore, strengthened the norms for public issues while retaining the freedom of the issuers to enter the new issues market and to freely price their issues. The disclosure standards were also strengthened for companies coming out with public issues for improving the levels of investor protection. Strict disclosure norms and entry point restrictions prescribed by SEBI made it difficult for most new companies without an established track record to access the public issues market. Whereas this helped to improve the quality of paper coming into the market, it contributed to a decline in the number of issues and the amount mobilised from the market.

Free-rider Paradox: Sometimes benefits and costs cannot be allocated accurately or at all to users by the markets or otherwise. A free rider tries to take advantage of this situation. The paradox is that if everyone tries to free ride no one can and everyone is worse off. An important example is the natural environment. Most industrial users of the natural environment are free riders. Everyone collectively is worse off but no one individually finds it worthwhile to stop. In takeovers, an important recent example is the basic research part of corporate research and development. It is impossible to limit the benefits from basic research to the corporation who pays the bill. Therefore, there will be a strong temptation for companies to free ride. Competition in the product and takeover market should increase this temptation.

Front Running: An unethical practice where brokers trade an equity based on information from the analysis department before their clients have been given the information. Fund manager/broker buys or sells securities in advance of a substantial client order.

Fungible Securities: Securities which are easily interchangeable with another in the same class.

Futures/Future Contracts: Future markets are designed to solve the problems that exist in forward markets. A future contract is an agreement between two parties to buy or sell an asset at a certain time in future at a certain price. However, unlike forward contracts, the future contracts are standardised and exchange traded. To facilitate liquidity in the future contracts, the exchange specifies certain standard features of the contract. It is a standardised contract with standard underlying instrument, a standard quantity and quality of the underlying instrument that can be delivered and a standard timing of such settlement.

A future contract may be offset prior to maturity by entering into an equal and opposite transaction. The standardised items in a future contract are as under:

1. Quantity of the underlying.
2. Quality of the underlying.
3. Date and the month of delivery.
4. Units of price quotation and minimum price change.
5. Location of settlement.

Future contracts are normally traded on an exchange. To make trading possible, the exchange specifies certain standardized features of the contract. As the two parties to the contract do not necessarily know each other the exchange also provides a mechanism, which gives the two parties a guarantee that the contract will be honoured.

Distinction between Futures and Forwards: Forward and future contracts are different in following respects.

Standardization: A forward contract is a tailor-made contract between the buyer and the seller where the terms are settled in mutual agreement between the parties. On the other hand, a future contract is standardized in regards to the quality, quantity, place of delivery of the asset etc. Only the price is negotiated. Forwards are popular on the over the counter (OTC) market. Futures are traded on an organised stock exchange. Exchange-traded derivatives tend to be more standardised and offer greater liquidity than OTC contracts, which are negotiated between counterparties and tailored to meet the needs of the parties to the contract. Exchange-traded derivatives also offer centralised limits on individual positions and have formal rules for risk and burden sharing.

Liquidity: There is no secondary market for forward contracts while future contracts are traded on organized exchanges. Accordingly, future contracts are usually much more liquid than the forward contracts. Forwards have customised contract terms, and therefore they are less liquid. Futures have standardised contract terms, and hence they are more liquid.

Conclusion of Contract: A forward contract is generally concluded with a delivery of the asset in question whereas the future contracts are settled sometimes with delivery of the asset and generally with the payment of the price differences. One who holds a contract can always eliminate his/her obligation by subsequently selling a contract for the same asset and same delivery date, before the conclusion of contract one holds. In the same manner, the seller of a future contract can buy a similar contract and offset his/her position before maturity of the first contract. Each one of these actions is called offsetting a trade.

Margins: A forward contract has zero value for both the parties involved so that no collateral is required for entering into such a contract. There are only two parties involved. But in a futures contract, a third party called clearing corporation, is also involved with which margin is required to be kept by both parties. In other words, forwards require no margin payments. Futures require margin payments.

Profit/Loss Settlement: The settlement of a forward contract takes place on the date of maturity so that the profit/loss is booked on maturity only. On the other hand, the future contracts are marked-to-market daily so that the profits or losses are settled daily. In other words, in the case of forwards, settlement happens at the end of the period. Futures follow daily settlement.

Thus, future contracts are a significant improvement over forward contracts as they eliminate counterparty risk and offer more liquidity.

Future contracts represent an improvement over the forward contracts in terms of standardization, performance guarantee and liquidity. A future contract is a standardized contract between two parties where one of the parties commits to sell, and the other to buy, a stipulated quantity of a commodity, currency, security, index or some other specified item at an agreed price on a given date in the future.

Future contracts are traded on commodity exchanges or other future exchanges. People can buy or sell futures like other commodities. When an investor buys a future contract on an organized future exchange, he is in fact assuming the right and obligation of taking the delivery of the specified underlying item on a specified date. Similarly, when an investor sells a contract, to take a short position, one assumes the right and obligation to make the delivery of the underlying asset. There is no risk of non-performance in the case of trading in the future contracts. This is because a clearing house or a clearing corporation is associated with the futures exchange, which plays a pivotal role in the trading of futures. A clearing house takes the opposite in each trade, so that it becomes the buyer to the seller and vice versa. When a party takes a short position in a contract, it is obliged to sell the underlying commodity in question at the stipulated price to the clearing house on maturity of the contract. Similarly, an investor who takes a long position on the contract can seek its performance through the clearing house only.

It is noteworthy that while a clearing house guarantees the performance of the future contracts, the parties in the contracts are required to keep margins with it. The margins are taken to ensure that each party to a contract performs its part. The margins are adjusted on a daily basis to account for the gains or losses, depending upon the situation. This is known as marking-to-market and involves giving a credit to the buyer of the contract, if the price of the contract rises, debiting the seller's account by an equal amount. Similarly, the buyer's balance is reduced when the contract price declines and the seller's account is accordingly updated.

It is not necessary to hold on to a futures contract until maturity and one can easily close out a position. Either of the parties may reverse their position by initiating a reverse trade, so that the original buyer of a contract can sell an identical contract at a later date, cancelling, in effect, the original contract. Thus, the exchange facilitates subsequent selling (buying) of a contract so that a party can offset its position and eliminate the obligation. The fact that the buyer as well as the seller of a contract is free to transfer his interest in the contract to another party makes such contracts highly liquid in nature. In fact, most of the future contracts are cancelled by the parties, by engaging into reverse trades: the buyers cancel a contract by selling another contract, while the seller does so by buying another contract. Only a very small portion of them is held for actual delivery.

Introduction of Futures in India: The first derivative product introduced in the Indian securities market was *index futures* in June 2000. In India, the *stock futures* were first introduced on November 9, 2001.

The Indian capital market has grown quite well since the early 1990s. In the boom period of 1992 and thereafter, even the common man was attracted to the stock market. The stock market was considered a profitable investment opportunity. Before July 2001, various stock exchanges including the Bombay Stock Exchange (BSE), National Stock Exchange (NSE) and Delhi stock Exchange, provided carry forward facilities through the traditional *badla* system. By means of this system the purchase or sale of a security was not postponed till a particular future date; instead the system only provided for the carry forward of a transaction from one settlement period (seven days) to the next settlement period for the payment of a fee known as *badla* charges.

In the *badla* system, due to limited settlement period and no future price discovery, a speculator could manipulate prices, thus causing loss to small investors and ultimately eroding investors' confidence in the capital market. Hence, the necessity of futures trading in the capital market was emphasized. In the absence of an efficient futures market, there was no price discovery and therefore prices could be moved in any desired direction. Recent developments in the capital market culminated in a ban on *badla* from July 2001.

In the absence of futures trading, certain operators—either on their own or in collusion with corporate management teams—at times manipulated prices in the secondary market, causing irreparable damage to the growth of the market. The small and medium investors, who are the backbone of the market and whose savings come to the market via primary or secondary routes shied away. As the small investors avoided the capital market, the downturn in the secondary market ultimately affected the primary market because people stopped investing in share for fear of loss or liquidity. Introducing futures in major shares along with index futures helped to revive the capital market. This not only provided liquidity and efficiency to the market, but also helped in future price discovery.

Futures and Stock Indices: For understanding stock index futures a thorough knowledge of the composition of indexes is essential. Choosing the right index is important in choosing the right contract for speculation or hedging. For speculation, the volatility of the index is important whereas for hedging the choice of index depends upon the relationship between the stocks being hedged and the characteristics of the index.

Choosing and understanding the right index is important as the movement of stock index futures is quite similar to that of the underlying stock index. Volatility of the future indexes is generally greater than spot stock indexes.

Every time an investor takes a long or short position on a stock, he also has hidden exposure to the Nifty or Sensex. This is so because most often stock values fall in tune with the entire market sentiment and rise when the market as a whole is rising.

Retail investors will find the index derivatives useful due to the high correlation of the index with their portfolio/stock and low cost associated with using index futures for hedging.

Index Futures: A future contract is an agreement between two parties to buy or sell an asset at a certain time in the future at a certain price. Index futures are all future contracts where the underlying is the stock index (Nifty or Sensex) and helps a trader to take a view of the market as a whole.

Index futures permit speculation and if a trader anticipates a major rally in the market, he can simply buy a future contract and hope for a price rise on the future contract when the rally occurs.

Settlements in the Futures Market: All trades in the futures market are cash settled on a T+1 basis and all positions (buy/sell) which are not closed out are marked-to-market. The closing price of the index futures is the daily settlement price and the position is carried to the next day at the settlement price.

The most common way of liquidating an open position is to execute an offsetting future transaction by which the initial transaction is squared up. The initial buyer liquidates his long position by selling identical future contract. In index futures the other way of settlement is cash settled at the final settlement. At the end of the contract period the difference between the contract value and closing index value is paid.

Gg

Gilt-edged Security: A term used to describe a bond, generally issued by the government, or issued with a government guarantee, so much so that there are no doubts about the ability of the issuer to pay regular interest and the principal amount to the bond holders.

Gilt Fund: It is a fund that invests exclusively in government securities.

Global Depository Receipt (GDR): Any instrument in the form of a depository receipt or certificate (by whatever name it is called) created by the Overseas Depository Bank outside India and issued to non-resident investors against the issue of ordinary shares or foreign currency convertible bonds of issuing company.

Global Financial Integration: It refers to the opening up of domestic markets and institutions to the free cross-border flow of capital and financial services by removing barriers such as capital controls and withholding taxes. A deeper dimension of global integration entails removing obstacles to movement of people, technology and market participants across border. Global integration is promoted through harmonisation of national standards and laws, either through the adoption of commonly agreed minimum standards or the mutual recognition of standards.

GLOBEX: A global after-hours electronic trading system.

Golden Handcuffs: A contract between a broker and brokerage house, offering lucrative commissions, bonuses and other benefits as long as the broker stays with the firm. Upon leaving, the broker must return much of the compensation.

Golden Parachute: A generous compensation contract awarded by the management to themselves in the anticipation of a takeover.

Good Delivery: Proper delivery by a seller to the buyer of the securities without any defect so that they can be transferred without any additional documentation.

Government Securities: Under Section 2 of the Securities Contracts (Regulation) Act, 1956, securities include the following:

1. Shares, scrips, stocks, bonds, debentures, debenture stocks, or other marketable securities of a like nature in or of any incorporated company or other body corporate.
2. Government securities.
3. Such other instruments as may be declared by the Central Government to be securities.
4. Rights or interests in securities.

Government Securities mean securities created and issued—whether before or after the commencement of the Securities Contracts (Regulations) Act, 1956—by the Central Government or a State Government for the purpose of raising a public loan and having one of the forms specified in Section 2(2) of the Public Debt Act, 1944 (since replaced by the Government Securities Act, 2006).

Markets for government securities have gained importance in many countries in the overall financial system in recent years. Initiatives have been taken to make them more vibrant and active by: (a) improving liquidity and depth, (b) enhancing transparency of primary issuances, (c) widening investor base, (d) fine-tuning auction procedures, (e) developing new instruments, and (f) putting in place appropriate safeguards and sound trading and settlement infrastructure. Furthermore, managers of public debt across countries are paying greater attention to minimising the cost of borrowings in the medium to long-term, while striking a balance between the costs and the risks in the short-run.

In India, the government securities market has witnessed significant transformation in its various dimensions, viz. market-based price discovery, widening of the investor base, introduction of new instruments, establishment of primary dealers and electronic trading and settlement infrastructure. This is the outcome of persistent and high-quality reforms in developing the government securities market. There are still areas where further development needs to be undertaken. Increased transparency and disclosures, gradual scaling down of mandated instruments and development of newer instruments are some major areas which could be considered. Regulatory incentives to increase the size of the trading book could be considered as a measure to further develop the government securities market.

Presently, investor base includes not only banks and insurance companies, but also private companies, private mutual funds, finance companies and individuals. Keeping this in view, a number of reform measures were initiated in this segment, which had a positive impact on both the primary and the secondary markets. Reforms in the government securities market have been introduced to impart liquidity and depth to the market by widening the investor base and by ensuring market-clearing interest rate mechanisms. See also Securities.

Grave Dancer: An acquirer who searches for bargains often among companies in dire financial straits or in bankruptcy.

Grey Market: It refers to a market in which commodities in short supply are sold for immediate delivery at exorbitant prices, taking unfair advantage of a crisis situation.

Gross Spread: The difference (spread) between a security's public offering price and the price paid to the issuer by an underwriter.

Growth Fund: Unit trusts or mutual funds which invest with the objective of achieving mostly capital growth rather than income. Growth funds are mostly more volatile than conservative income or money market funds because managers invest in shares that are subject to larger price movements.

Guarantor: A party who agrees to be responsible for the payment of another party's debts should that party default.

Hh

Hammering the Market: Intensive sale of stocks to drive prices down.

Hedge: An asset, liability or financial commitment that protects against adverse changes in the value of or cash flows from another investment or liability. An unhedged investment or liability is called an *exposure*.

Hedgers: Hedgers are the traders who wish to eliminate the risk (of price change) to which they are already exposed. They may take a long position on, or short sell, a commodity and would, therefore, stand to lose should the prices move in the adverse direction. The trader can sell future (or forward) contracts with a matching price, to hedge.

Stocks carry two types of risk: company specific and market risk. While company risk can be minimized by diversifying portfolio, market risk cannot be diversified but has to be hedged.

Hedging: It is the process of stabilizing the value (including cash flows) of a given portfolio by neutralizing adverse market movements. Hedging involves protecting an existing asset position from future adverse price movements. In order to hedge a position, a market player needs to take an equal and opposite position in the futures market to the one held in the cash market.

Held for Trading (HFT): Holding securities with the intention to trade by taking advantage of short-term price/interest rate movements.

Held Till Maturity (HTM): Securities acquired by the banks with the intention to hold them up to maturity.

Horizontal Spread: The purchase of either a call or put option and the simultaneous sale of the same type of option with typically the same strike price but with a different expiration month. Also referred to as calendar spread.

Hostile Bid: An effort to gain control of a target company that has not been agreed to by the target's management and board, usually through a tender offer or an unsolicited proposal to the board. Sometimes called an unsolicited bid.

Hot Issue: A security that is expected to trade in the after market at a premium over the public offering price.

Hot Money: Short-term international capital movements, motivated by interest rate differential or revaluation hopes/devaluation fears.

Hybrid: Any security which has the character of more than one type of security, including their derivatives.

Hypothecation: Pledging assets against a loan. The ownership of the asset or the income from the asset is not transferred, except that in default of repayment of loan the asset may be sold to realize its value. Brokers will accept shares as collateral for loans to finance purchase of shares or to cover short sales.

Ii

Index Fund: A mutual fund which invests in a portfolio of shares that matches identically the constituents of a well-known stock market index. Hence, changes in the value of the fund mirror changes in the index itself.

Indexed Asset: An indexed asset has coupon and principal payments that are adjusted upward in response to increase in price level. This adjustment is intended to compensate lenders for the decline in purchasing power of loan repayments.

India Brand Equity Foundation (IBEF): It is a public-private partnership between the Ministry of Commerce and Industry, Government of India and the Confederation of Indian Industry (CII). It collects, collates and disseminates comprehensive and current information on the Indian economy and business. www.ibef.org has been developed as a single-window resource for in-depth information and insight on India. IBEF also produces a wide range of well-researched publications focused on India's economic and business advantages.

Indian Depository Receipt: A receipt, evidencing an underlying foreign security, issued in India by a foreign company which has entered into an agreement with the issuer and depository, custodian and depository or underwriters and depository, in accordance with the terms of prospectus or letter of offer, as may be prescribed.

Initial Margin: The initial amount which customers have to put in before taking up a futures contract to guarantee the transaction.

Initial Public Offering (IPO): The first public issue by a public limited company.

Inside Quote: The highest bid and lowest ask prices among all the competing market makers in a security, i.e. the best bid and offer prices.

Insider: Any person who is or was connected with the company or is deemed to have been connected with the company, and who is reasonably expected to have access, connection to unpublished price sensitive information in respect of securities of a company, or who has received or has had access to such unpublished price sensitive information.

Insider Trading: Practice of corporate agents buying or selling their corporation's securities without disclosing to the public significant information which is known to them but which has not yet affected the price.

Institutional Investors: Organizations which invest, including insurance companies, depository institutions, pension funds, investment companies, and endowment funds.

Institutionalization: The gradual domination of financial markets by institutional investors, as opposed to individual investors. This process has occurred throughout the industrialized world.

Insurance Regulatory and Development Authority (IRDA): The supervisory control of insurance companies in India is exercised by IRDA and these powers flow from Insurance Act, 1938 as well as from IRDA Act, 1999. IRDA Act, 1999 states: "Subject to the provisions of this Act and any other law for the time being in force, the Authority shall have the duty to regulate, promote and ensure orderly growth of insurance business and reinsurance business". Regulatory and supervisory powers of the IRDA are wide and pervasive.

Intangible Assets: An item of value whose true worth is hard or almost impossible to determine such as goodwill, reputation, patents and so on.

Inter-corporate Dividends: These are dividends received by a company from another company. Income tax laws generally treat a parent (or a holding) company and its subsidiary company as separate legal entities and therefore tax them separately. Thus, if a holding company receives dividends from its subsidiary, the former has to pay tax on such dividends. Taxation of inter-corporate earnings is designed to prevent concentration of economic power in the hands of corporate giants. However, this provision is said to give rise to treble taxation of such dividends, first in the hands of the earning company, then in the hands of the receiving company, and finally in the hands of individual shareholders. Tax laws often provide certain concessions to facilitate inter-corporate investment.

In India, prior to the assessment year 1991-92, the adverse situation was partially remedied by Section 80M of the Income Tax Act, 1961, under which a company was entitled to a deduction of 60 percent of dividend received by it from another domestic company. An important change was introduced from the assessment year 1991-92 under which dividends received by a domestic company from another domestic company are now exempt to the full extent to which the assessee company itself distributes dividends during the relevant period. Business community has complained that this arrangement has forced companies to declare dividends. It favours complete exemption of inter-corporate dividends from tax.

Inter-delivery Spread: The purchase of one delivery month of a given futures contract and simultaneous sale of another delivery month of the same contract on the same exchange. Also called intra-market spread.

Interest Rate Agreement: An agreement whereby one party, for an upfront premium, agrees to compensate the other at specific time periods if a designated interest rate (the reference rate) is different from a pre-determined level (the strike rate).

Interest Rate Cap: An interest rate agreement in which payments are made when the reference rate exceeds the strike rate. Also called an interest rate ceiling.

Interest Rate Differential: The difference between the existing rate of interest and the rate for the term remaining, multiplied by the principal outstanding and the balance of the term.

Interest Rate Forward Contracts: Non-standardised, non-listed agreements typically bought and sold by individuals or corporations that are often connected by ongoing business relations.

Interest Rate Futures: Financial futures that are considered to be primarily sensitive to interest rate movements.

Interest Rate Hedges: Position designed to restrict losses that would occur from specific interest rate movements.

Interest Rate Risk: The risk that movements in the interest rates may lead to a change in expected return.

Interest Rate Swap: Contract in which two parties agree to swap interest payments for a pre-determined period of time traded in the OTC market.

Interim Dividend: A dividend payment made during the course of a company's financial year. Interim dividend, unlike the final dividend, does not have to be agreed in a general meeting.

Internal Capital Adequacy Assessment Process (ICAAP): In terms of the guidelines on BASEL II, the banks are required to have a board-approved policy on ICAAP to assess the capital requirement as per ICAAP at the solo as well as consolidated level. The ICAAP is required to form an integral part of the management and decision-making culture of a bank. ICAAP document is required to clearly demarcate the quantifiable and qualitatively assessed risks. The ICAAP is also required to include stress tests and scenario analyses, to be conducted periodically, particularly in respect of the bank's material risk exposures. This is necessary to evaluate the potential vulnerability of the bank to some unlikely but plausible events or movements in the market conditions that could have an adverse impact on the bank's capital.

Internal Rate of Return (IRR): The rate at which future cash flows must be discounted in order to equal the cash cost of the investment.

International Securities Identification Number (ISIN): A unique identification number allotted for each security in the depository system by SEBI.

International Swaps and Derivatives Association (ISDA): It promotes orderly practices in the swap market, conducts research on the volume and quality of transactions, and public understanding. ISDA, established in 1985, is a not-for-profit corporation, with headquarters in New York City. Its members include over 140 institutions worldwide representing dealers in swaps, corporations, software firms, and law firms. ISDA, formerly known as the International Swap Dealers Association, changed its name in August 1993.

In-the-money: A call option is said be in the money when it has a strike price below the current price of the underlying commodity or security on which the option has been written. Likewise, when a put option has a strike price above the current price it is said to be in-the-money.

In-the-money Option: An in-the-money option is an option that would lead to a positive cash flow to the holder if it were exercised immediately. A call option on the index is said to be in-the-money when the current value of index stands at a level higher than the strike price (i.e. spot price > strike price). If the value of index is much higher than the strike price, the call is said to be deep in-the-money. On the other hand, a put option on index is said to be in-the-money if the value of index is below the strike price.

Investment Banker: Financial conglomerate which conducts a full range of investment-related activities from advising clients on securities issues, acquisitions and disposal of businesses, arranging and underwriting new securities, distributing the securities etc.

Investment Commission (IC): The three-member Investment Commission, set up in the Ministry of Finance in December 2004 by the Government of India, has Mr. Ratan Tata as Chairman and Mr. Deepak Parekh and Dr. Ashok Ganguly as members. It: (a) advises the Government of India on changes in policy and procedures that will enhance investment in India, (b) recommends projects and investment proposals that should be fast-tracked/monitored, and (c) promotes India as an investment destination.

Investment Company: A corporation, trust or partnership that invests pooled unit holder/shareholder money in securities appropriate to the organization's objective. Mutual funds, close-ended funds and unit investment trusts are the three types of investment companies.

Investor Protection Fund (IPF): The stock exchanges have put in place a system for redressal of investors' grievances for matters relating to trading members and companies. They ensure that critical and price-sensitive information reaching the exchange is made available to all classes of investor at the same point of time. Further, to protect the interests of investors, IPF has also been set up by the stock exchanges. The exchanges maintain an IPF to take care of investor claims, which may arise out of non-settlement of obligations by the trading member, who has been declared a defaulter, in respect of trades executed on the exchange. Measures of investor protection that have been put in place over the reform period have led to increased confidence among investors. To improve the availability of information to investors, all listed companies are required to publish unaudited financial results on a quarterly basis.

A continuing increase in the savings rate of households suggests that there is no supply constraint in terms of financial resources that could be channelled into the equity market. After the exuberance of the stock market in the mid-1990s and its decline thereafter, a large number of individual investors took flight to safety in bank deposits, safe retirement instruments and insurance. Households in India have increasingly tended to prefer savings in the form of safe and contractual instruments as opposed to capital market based instruments. Although retail investors have started showing some increased interest in the equity market in recent years, there is a need to increase their participation further.

Jj

Jitney: It describes a situation where one broker who has direct access to a stock exchange performs trades for a broker who does not have access. It is a kind of fraudulent activity in the penny stock market. It occurs when two brokers work together by trading a stock back and forth to rack up commissions and give the impression of trading volume.

Jobbers: Member brokers of a stock exchange who specialize, by giving two way quotations, in buying and selling of securities from and to fellow members. Jobbers do not have any direct contact with the public but they serve the useful function of imparting liquidity to the market.

Jobbers Spread: The difference between the price at which a jobber is prepared to sell and the price at which he is prepared to buy. A large difference reflects an imbalance between supply and demand.

Joint Liability Group (JLG): A JLG is an informal group comprising of 5 to 10 individual members who come together for the purpose of availing bank loans either individually or through the group mechanism against a mutual guarantee.

Micro finance sector caters to the needs of poor people and the loans given by micro finance institutions are not backed by any security (i.e. unsecured loans). As is well-known, unsecured loans are always risky because very little can be done if loans are not repaid. To meet this challenge micro finance institutions have adopted the concept of JLGs.

In a JLG, the borrowers make a group among themselves and the micro finance institution gives loan to the group. A person in that group is appointed as leader of the group and each person is responsible for the loan taken by any member of the group. If any one person in the group defaults then other group members will have to pay for that.

The Group concept is helpful because everyone is monitored by others in the group and the borrower utilises his money properly. If any one defaults, other group members will make all possible efforts to take money back from him. This arrangement motivates the borrowers to maintain discipline while asking for loan and utilising it appropriately. It is possible that sometimes the group also defaults. However, it is a different problem which is less likely to occur. JLG concept helps the micro finance institutions to reduce the default risk. Moreover, it inculcates the habit of disciplined management of finance among the poor.

The National Bank for Agriculture and Rural Development (NABARD) is operating a joint liability group (JLG) scheme to provide access to institutional credit to small, marginal, tenant farmers, oral lessees and share croppers.

Joint Venture (JV): An Indian entity incorporated in accordance with the laws and regulations in India in whose capital a non-resident entity makes an investment.

Junk Bond: High yield bond issued by low-rated companies.

Kk

Kapli: A standard form used by the broker to inform the stock exchange of his transactions for the purpose of matching a settlement.

Key Currency Country: It refers to the country whose currency is used world-wide as a reserve asset as well as for undertaking trade transactions. US is one such country whose national currency, namely dollar is functioning as an international key currency. The advantage to US is that it is exempt from pressures of balance of payments deficit. It need not reduce its gold stock or its stock of foreign currency reserves as long as its foreign trading partners remain willing to accumulate balances in key currency (dollar) rather than to sell it in foreign exchange market. Thus, there will be no pressure on dollar to fall below its given exchange rate in response to the deficit.

Ll

Lagging Indicators: Market indicators showing the general direction of the economy and confirming or denying the trend implied by the leading indicators or concurrent indicators.

Lame Duck: A defaulter on a stock exchange who is not able to meet his market commitment and financial obligations of his business.

Law of One Price: An economic rule stating that a given security must have the same price regardless of the means by which one goes about creating that security. This implies that if the payoff of a security can be synthetically created by a package of other securities, the price of the package and the price of the security whose payoff it replicates must be equal.

Lay Off: The sell off by an issuer of any or all unsubscribed shares in a rights offering to the underwriters at the subscription price.

Lead Manager: The merchant banker associated with the issue and responsible for due diligence and other associated issue- related activities.

Legal Risk: The risk of loss because a law or regulation is applied in an unexpected way or because a contract cannot be enforced.

Letter of Offer: A letter of offer is a document addressed to the shareholders of the target company containing disclosures of the acquirer, target company, justification of the offer price, the offer price, number of shares to be acquired from the public, purpose of acquisition, future plans of acquirer etc.

Liabilities: Any claim for money against the assets of a company, such as bills of creditors, income tax payable, debenture redemption, interest on secured and unsecured loans etc. Although on balance sheet shareholders' equity is shown under liability, it has no claim on the assets of a company, unless it goes into liquidation.

Limited Liability Partnership (LLP) Act, 2008: Recently the Limited Liability Partnership (LLP) Act, 2008 has been enacted which provides for a flexible governance structure to be determined by the partners themselves by mutual agreement, easy compliance requirements in comparison to companies, combined with limitation of liability to the .extent of the partners contribution. It paves the way for greater corporatisation of the small and medium enterprises, thereby enhancing their access to equity and funds from the market.

The salient features of the LLP Act, 2008 are as under:

1. LLP shall be a body corporate and a legal entity separate from its partners. It will have perpetual succession. Indian Partnership Act, 1932 shall not be applicable to LLPs, since LLP shall be in the form of a body corporate.
2. An LLP has to be incorporated with a minimum of two persons. The Act does not restrict the benefit of LLP structure to certain classes of professionals only and would be available for use by any enterprise which fulfils the requirements of the Act.
3. The LLP will be an alternative corporate business vehicle that would give the benefits of limited liability but would allow its members the flexibility of organizing their internal structure as a partnership based on an agreement.
4. On registration LLP shall be capable of: (a) suing and being sued, and (b) acquiring, owning, holding and developing or disposing off property.
5. A person may cease to be a partner of a LLP in accordance with an agreement with the other partners or in absence of agreement with the other partners, by giving a notice in writing of not less than 30 days of his intention to resign as partner.
6. In the event of an act carried out by a LLP, or any of its partners, with intend to defraud creditors of the LLP or any other person or for any fraudulent purpose, the liability of the LLP and partners, who acted with intend to defraud creditors or for

any fraudulent purpose shall be unlimited for all or any of the debts or other liabilities of the LLP.

7. A contribution of a partner may consist of tangible, movable or immovable or intangible property or other benefits to the LLP including money, promissory notes, other agreements to contribute cash or property, and contracts for services performed or to be performed.
8. While the LLP will be a separate legal entity, liable to the full extent of its assets, the liability of the partners would be limited to their agreed contribution in the LLP. Further, no partner would be liable on account of the independent or unauthorized actions of other partners, thus allowing individual partners to be shielded from joint liability created by another partner's wrongful business decisions or misconduct.
9. An LLP shall be under obligation to maintain annual accounts reflecting true and fair view of its state of affairs.
10. Provisions have been made in the Act for corporate actions like mergers, amalgamations etc.
11. There is a provision of voluntary winding up as well as winding up by the Tribunal.
12. There are provisions for inter conversion of LLP into private company etc.

Line Business: Brokers who have teleprints in their offices communicate the quantity, price etc., as soon as deals are struck, for onward transmission to their branch offices. This is known as line business. It also includes arbitrage.

Liquid Assets: Liquid assets consists of cash, balances with RBI, balances in current accounts with banks, money at call and short notice, inter-bank placements due within 30 days and securities under *held for trading* and *available for sale* categories, excluding securities that do not have ready market.

Liquidation: The process of converting stocks into cash. Also means the dissolution of a company.

Liquidity Premium: Additional return required to compensate investors for purchasing illiquid assets.

Liquidity Risk: The risk that a solvent institution is temporarily unable to meet its monetary obligations.

Listed Company: A company which has any of its securities, offered through an offer document, listed on a recognised stock exchange and also includes public sector undertakings whose securities are listed on a recognised stock exchange.

Listing: It means formal admission of a security into a public trading system.

Listing Agreement: An agreement which has to be entered into by companies when they seek listing for their shares on a stock exchange. Companies are called upon to keep the stock exchange fully informed of all corporate developments—like dividend, rights, bonus shares etc.—having a bearing on the market price of shares.

***Lok Adalats* (Peoples Courts):** In the area of dispute settlement, the Legal Services Authority Act, 1987 has conferred statutory basis on the *Lok Adalats*. The RBI issued guidelines to commercial banks and financial institutions to enable them to make increasing use of the forum of *Lok Adalats*. In terms of the guidelines, banks could settle banking disputes involving an amount up to ₹ 5 lakh through the forum of *Lok Adalats*. The Central Government, in consultation with the RBI, decided to increase the monetary ceiling of cases to be referred to the *Lok Adalats* organised by Civil Courts. Accordingly, on August 3, 2004, the RBI enhanced the monetary ceiling of cases to be referred to *Lok Adalats* organised by Civil Courts to ₹ 20 lakh as against the earlier ceiling of ₹ 5 lakh.

London Inter-bank Offer Rate (LIBOR): Often used as a basis for pricing Euroloans, LIBOR represents the interest rate at which first class banks in London are prepared to offer dollar deposits to other first class banks. There are similar rates like Hong Kong Inter-bank Offer Rate (HIBOR); Singapore Inter-bank Offer Rate (SIBOR); Toronto Inter-bank Offer Rate (TIBOR); and Mumbai Inter-bank Bid and Offer Rates (MIBOR) (q.v).

Long Position: A position showing a purchase or a greater number of purchases than sales in anticipation of a rise in prices. A long position can be closed out through the sale of an equivalent amount.

Loss Asset: A loss asset is one where loss has been identified by the bank or internal or external auditors or the RBI inspection but the amount has not been written off wholly. In other words, such an asset is considered uncollectible and of such little value that its continuance as a bankable asset is not warranted although there may be some salvage or recovery value.

Mm

Margin: An advance payment of a portion of the value of a stock transaction. The amount of credit a broker or lender extends to a customer for stock purchase.

Margin Call: In the process of marking-to-the-market, if the balance in the margin account falls below the maintenance margin, the investor receives a margin call and is required to deposit additional funds to bring the balance to the level of initial margin in a very short period of time. The extra funds deposited are called variation margin.

Markdown: A charge levied by a broker when buying securities on its own account from a customer.

Marked-to-market Basis: The process whereby the book value or collateral value of a security is adjusted to reflect current market value.

Market Capitalization: The market value of a company, calculated by multiplying the number of shares issued and outstanding by their current market price.

Market Discipline: Market discipline seeks to achieve increased transparency through expanded disclosure requirements for banks.

Market if Touched (MIT): A limit order that automatically becomes a market order if the price is reached.

Market Maker: A member firm which gives two way quotation for particular security(ies) and which is under obligation to buy and sell them subject to certain conditions such as overall exposure, spread etc.

Market Order: An order to buy or sell a contract at whatever price is available at the time of entering the order on the system.

Market Risk: Market risk is defined as the risk of loss arising from movements in market prices or rates away from the rates or prices set out in a transaction or agreement.

Market Watch: The purpose of market watch is to allow continuous monitoring of contracts or securities that are of specific interest to the user. It displays trading information for contracts selected by the user. The user also gets a broadcast of all the cash market securities on the screen. This function is also available if the user selects the relevant securities for display on the market watch screen. Display of trading information related to cash market securities is in *read only* format, i.e. the dealer can only view the information on cash market but cannot trade in them through the system. This is the main window from the dealer's perspective.

Marketable Lot: Also called unit of trading, it refers to a fixed minimum number, in which or in multiples of which, shares are bought and sold on the stock exchange. For shares whose face value is ₹ 10, the marketable or trading lot may be 50 or 100. For ₹ 100 shares the market lot is usually 5 or 10. Companies may, however, decide on other lots, such as 1 share for ₹ 500, although it is now rare. Any number of share less than the marketable lot makes an odd lot. In other words, anything less than the standard unit of trading is odd lot. It is difficult to buy and disadvantageous to sell odd lots. When companies issue bonus or rights shares in less than 1:1 ratio, odd lots are often the result.

Marking-to-market: In the futures market, at the end of each trading day, the margin account is adjusted to reflect the investor's gain or loss depending upon the futures closing price. This is called marking-to-market.

Marking-up Prices: Prices fixed by the stock exchange to facilitate settlement of bargains in the specified securities, particularly at the end of the settlement period.

Mark-up: A charge levied by a broker when selling securities from its own account to a customer. These sales as principals to a customer take place at the best ask price plus a commission equivalent to mark-up.

MAT: See Minimum Alternative Tax, *132*.

Matched Transaction: A check is carried out on the computer to find out whether purchases and sales as reported by the members match. The transactions, thus compared are called matched transactions.

Maturity Date: The date on which a loan, bond, or debenture becomes due for payment.

Maturity Value: The amount an investor receives when a security is redeemed at maturity, not including any periodic interest payments.

Merchant Banker: Any person who is engaged in the business of issue management, either by making arrangement regarding selling, buying or subscribing to securities or acting as manager, consultant, adviser or rendering corporate advisory service in relation to such issue management.

Merger: The non-hostile and voluntary union of two companies.

Micro Credit: See Micro Finance, *128*.

Micro Finance: Micro finance is the provision of a diverse range of financial services and products including small loans (micro credit), savings accounts, insurance, pensions and money transfers. These are designed to assist people living in poverty who are not able to access financial services in the mainstream banking sector because they have no collateral, formal identification or steady income.

The proposed Micro Finance Services Regulation Bill defines micro finance services as providing financial assistance to an individual or an eligible client, either directly or through a group mechanism for an amount, not exceeding ₹ 50,000 in aggregate (₹ 1,50,000 if for housing purposes).

Salient Features of Micro Finance: These are as under:

1. Borrowers are from the low-income group.
2. Loans are of small amount.
3. Loans are for short duration.
4. Loans are offered without collaterals.
5. Loans are generally given for income generation purpose.
6. Repayment frequency is high.
7. Loan terms vary, but once repaid, the money is recycled and lent out to someone else.

Micro Finance and Micro Credit Distinguished: Micro finance is different from micro credit. Micro finance is a broad category of services, which includes micro credit. Micro credit is provision of credit services to poor clients. Micro credit is one of the aspects of micro finance and the two are often confused. Under micro credit, small amounts of loans are given to the borrower but under micro finance besides loans many other financial services are provided such as savings account, insurance etc. Therefore, micro finance is a wider concept as compared to micro credit.

Micro credit is the provision of small, collateral-free loans to people living in poverty to use as business capital. Loans are used to start or grow micro enterprises that help give them a regular income—whether it is a small farm, food stall, jewellery-making business or taxi. They may use loans to buy stock or equipment, creating a sustainable livelihood for themselves and their families. Through the profits they earn, they are able to provide for their children and repay the loans over time.

Micro Finance and Allied Services: Apart from providing

small loans, micro finance also includes a range of financial services to the poor. Some of these are as follows.

***Savings Accounts*:** These are meant to help provide a safety net in times of need and help to plan for the future. Without an alternative, people living in poverty hide their money in boxes under their beds or in holes in the ground. They also put their money into assets—such as livestock or pieces of jewellery, which offer little real security—they can be stolen, deteriorate or be destroyed by natural disasters.

Micro savings are deposit services offered by financial institutions that allow people living in poverty to securely store small amounts of money. Micro finance institutions offer savings facilities—some even make them compulsory, encouraging families to plan for unexpected expenses so they can have the freedom to invest in healthcare, education, housing and their businesses when the need arises.

In many cases, banking regulations do not allow micro finance institutions to directly offer micro savings services. Agency arrangements with banks can help overcome this problem.

***Micro Insurance*:** This is meant to protect against emergencies and disasters. Micro insurance is insurance for low-income households that protects against unforeseen events so that savings and working capital can be maintained rather than eroded. Like savings, it helps provide security against the many risks faced by those living in poverty.

Innovative products offered by micro finance institutions cover policyholders with crop, loan, health, life and property insurance—offering families a safety net when an unexpected hardship occurs so they are not forced back into poverty.

***Micro Pensions*:** Micro pensions are accumulation superannuation accounts. They are funded by an individual's contribution and, in some cases, a matched contribution from the government. They are meant to help provide an income in old age.

Fund Transfers and Remittance Products: These are meant to help families, living far apart, access their incomes. Money transfers are domestic and international electronic transfers of money. They are used for a variety of purposes, including regular bill payment, one-time-only money needs, delivering money from people working in urban areas to their family members in rural areas, and sending money from migrants to family members in their country of origin (remittances).

Many developing countries lack any viable money transfer services, and substantial volumes of global remittances continue to flow through informal and sometimes dangerous underground channels which are outside government supervision and regulation. Micro finance institutions are increasingly trying to seek alliances with banks and money transfer companies to offer safe, convenient and lower-cost transfers to their clients, many utilising mobile phone technologies.

Micro Finance Clients and Activities: Often, people do not have enough money when they face a need, so they borrow. A poor family might borrow from relatives to buy land, from a moneylender to buy rice, or from a micro finance institution to buy a sewing machine.

In urban areas, micro finance activities are diverse and include shopkeepers, service providers, artisans, street vendors, manufacturers and so on. In rural areas, they are typically small-scale farmers and others who are engaged in small income-generating activities such as food processing and trade.

Micro finance institutions (MFIs) have clients that run businesses such as convenience stores, bakeries, canteens, fruit and vegetable stalls or recycling shops. Others offer services in carpentry, transport, tailoring, food manufacturing or repairs, while many rural clients have small farms where they keep animals or produce crops such as rice.

A major incentive for clients to repay loans is their ability to secure subsequent, larger loans once initial loans are repaid. This enables entrepreneurs to grow their businesses more and more with each subsequent loan, increasing their productivity, income and the living standards of their family.

Borrowers often form guaranteeing groups, particularly in early loan cycles. This community approach provides support when an individual is unable to make a loan repayment, possibly due to illness or other hardship.

Businesses of clients are vulnerable to a range of factors. In most cases, MFIs provide information and basic business training to equip clients with the knowledge and skills they need to make the most of their loan.

People can use small loans to start businesses such as the following: tailoring shops, vegetable farms, small grocery stores, hairdressing saloons, bicycle repair shops, tea shops, pig breeding farms, basket weaving, rickshaw taxi services, clothing market stalls, fishing operations, construction businesses etc.

Micro Insurance: See Micro Finance, *128*.

Micro Pensions: See Micro Finance, *128*.

Minimum Alternative Tax (MAT): Income tax laws throughout the world generally provide for a number of tax concessions. A clever profit-making company may arrange its affairs in such a manner that the cumulative effect of all tax concessions is to reduce its income declared in the tax return to zero. MAT is a device to keep a Zero Tax Company (q.v.) within the tax net.

In India, if the income disclosed by a company in the tax return (after claiming all deductions) is less than 30 percent of its book profits then this 30 percent of the book profits is subject to tax. The concept of minimum alternative tax also prevails in the US where it is called alternative minimum tax (AMT). However, under its laws if in the subsequent years the company pays tax on its regular income (income declared in the tax return) then the minimum alternative tax paid earlier on its adjusted taxable income is allowed as a set off against the tax payable on regular income. In the US, AMT was designed as a part of the Tax Reform Act of 1986, in response to the concern that a number of firms that reported positive book profits paid no corporate tax to the Federal Government.

Money Laundering: It is the process of converting the proceeds of illegal activities—disclosure of which would trigger financial losses or criminal prosecution—into real or financial assets whose origins remain effectively hidden from law enforcement officials and from society in general.

Money Market: Money market is the most important segment of the financial system as it provides the fulcrum for equilibrating short-term demand for and supply of funds, thereby facilitating the conduct of monetary policy. It is a market for short-term funds with a maturity of up to one year and includes financial instruments that are close substitutes for money. The main instruments comprising the money market are the following:

1. Call Money Market (q.v.).
2. Certificates of Deposit (CDs) (q.v.).
3. Repurchase Agreements (repos) (q.v.).
4. Commercial Bills (q.v.).
5. Commercial Papers (CPs) (q.v.).
6. Collateralised Borrowing and Lending Obligation (CBLO) (q.v.)
7. Inter-corporate Funds.

While inter-bank money markets and central bank lending via repo operations or discounting, provide liquidity for banks, private non-bank money market instruments, such as commercial bills and commercial paper provide liquidity to the commercial sector. Unlike in developed economies where money markets are promoted by financial intermediaries out of efficiency considerations, in India, as in many other developing countries, the evolution of the money market and its structure has been integrated into the overall deregulation process of the financial sector.

The money market is generally expected to perform three broad functions.

1. It provides an equilibrating mechanism to even out demand for and supply of short-term funds.
2. It also presents a focal point for central bank intervention for influencing liquidity and general level of interest rates in the economy.

3. It provides reasonable access to providers and users of short-term funds to fulfil their borrowing and investment requirements at an efficient market clearing price.

The RBI is the most important constituent of the money market. Owing to its implications for conducting monetary policy, the money market falls under the direct purview of regulation of the RBI. The primary objective of the RBI's operations in the money market has been to ensure that short-term interest rates and liquidity are maintained at levels which are consistent with the overall monetary policy objectives, *viz.* maintaining price stability, ensuring adequate flow of credit to the productive sectors of the economy and maintaining orderly conditions in the financial markets. Liquidity and interest rates in the system are influenced by the RBI through the use of various instruments at its disposal which, *inter alia*, include the following.

1. Variations in cash reserve ratio.
2. Standing facilities/refinance schemes.
3. Repo and reverse repo transactions.
4. Changes in the bank rate.
5. Open market operations.
6. Foreign exchange swap operations.

Recognising the important role of the market in the monetary policy process, the RBI has taken active interest in continuously refining the money market instruments in order to have greater control over the liquidity in the system and for creating an efficient mechanism to impart interest rate signals.

Money Market Mutual Funds: Schemes investing exclusively in safer short-term instruments such as treasury bills, certificates of deposit, commercial paper and inter-bank call money, government securities etc.

Moral Hazard: The risk that a party to a transaction has not entered into a contract in good faith, has provided misleading information about its assets, liabilities or credit capacity or has an incentive to take unusual risks in a desperate attempt to avoid losses.

Mortgage: A debt instrument used in a real estate transaction where the property is the collateral for the loan. A mortgage gives the lender a right to take possession of the property if the borrower fails to pay off the loan.

Mortgage Trust: Unit trust which invests in mortgage loans. Effectively the unit trust invests money in real estate and receives an interest return with security over the property which has been purchased. The interest which is charged on mortgage trust loans is normally higher than that other sources of finance like banks so that the investor usually receives a very competitive rate or return.

Mortgage-backed Securities: Securities backed by mortgage loans, including pass-through securities, modified pass-through securities, mortgage-backed bonds, and mortgage pay-through securities.

Multinational Corporation: A multinational corporation (MNC) or transnational corporation is a large sized, dominant company involved in production and trade of a wide range of commodities or services and based in two or more countries. It consists of a parent company from where it emerged and where its ownership and management rest. In other countries, there are subsidiaries which are partly owned and managed by people of various nationalities. Large capital base, technological superiority, innovations, advertisements and an oligopolistic ownership have led to the growth of transnational corporation since the early 1960s.

Mumbai Inter-bank Bid and Offer Rates (MIBOR): Calculated by the average of the inter-bank offer rates based on quotations at nearly 30 major banks.

Mutual Funds: Mutual funds are very popular all over the world and they play an important role in the financial system of many countries. Mutual funds are an ideal medium for investment by small investors in the stock market. Mutual funds pool together the investments of small investors for participation in the stock market. Being institutional investors, mutual funds can afford market analysis generally not available to individual investors. Furthermore, mutual funds can diversify the portfolio in a better way as compared with individual investors due to the expertise and availability of funds.

Legal and Regulatory Framework: In general, the mutual fund regulatory framework in India is much more extensive and developed than in many other countries. Indian mutual funds are unit trusts, formed under the Indian Trusts Act of 1882. Their operation is governed by mutual fund regulations, totalling 78, promulgated by SEBI in exercise of the powers conferred by Section 30, read with clause (c) of sub-section (2) of section 11 of the Securities and Exchange Board of India, Act 1992. The first set of mutual fund regulations was originally promulgated in 1996, and has since been amended from time to time. In order to remove any difficulties in the application or interpretation of these regulations, Regulation 77 of the mutual funds regulations additionally authorises SEBI to issue "clarifications and guidelines in the form of notes or circulars which shall be binding upon the sponsor, mutual funds, trustees, asset management companies and custodians".

History of Mutual Funds: Mutual funds in India were first created in 1963 when the Unit Trust of India (UTI), a state-sponsored entity, came into being. Until 1987, UTI was the only mutual fund in the country. Between 1987 and 1993 other entities belonging to the public sector were permitted to offer mutual funds—basically state-controlled banks and insurers. As part of financial sector reforms, the mutual fund industry was opened to the private sector in 1993. Thus, from 1993 onwards, private sector organisations were permitted to enter the market and the first mutual fund regulations were promulgated, which were subsequently replaced by the SEBI (Mutual Fund) Regulations of 1996. These private sector organisations comprised both Indian and foreign joint ventures as well as purely Indian firms.

Since then, the expansion of mutual fund business has

intensified competition and led to product innovation. Mutual funds presently offer a variety of options to investors such as income funds, balanced funds, liquid funds, gift funds, index funds, exchange traded funds, sectoral funds etc. The deceleration in the growth of mutual funds in the 1990s could be attributed partly to the relatively poor performance of the stock markets and partly due to withdrawal of tax benefits under Section 80M of the Indian Income Tax Act, 1961. Some of the mutual funds had offered assured return schemes enabling them to mobilise large resources. A number of mutual funds faced difficulties in meeting their redemption obligations relating to such schemes. In several cases, the sponsors of mutual funds had to infuse additional funds to meet the shortfall. As a result, mutual funds, by and large, discontinued the floatation of assured return schemes, which had some dampening effect on the resource mobilisation by mutual funds.

Bifurcation of UTI: While most of the mutual funds were somehow able to meet their commitments on account of assured return schemes, UTI faced a somewhat different problem on two different occasions between October 1998 and July 2001. US-64, which was the flagship scheme of UTI and enjoyed the investors' faith, first faced problem in December 1998 when the reserves under the scheme were reported negative. In order to restore investors' confidence, several measures were initiated by the Government/UTI. While these measures helped the US-64 to make a turnaround, the problem resurfaced again in July 2001 when UTI slashed down the dividend rates for the year 2000-01 and suspended sales and repurchases of US-64 for a period of 6 months from July 2001 to December 2001. This created a crisis of confidence and to restore investors' confidence various measures were initiated again, which culminated in splitting the UTI into two parts.

On October 28, 2002, an ordinance was promulgated which repealed the UTI Act, and bifurcated UTI into two separate entities. One is the specified undertaking of the Unit Trust of India. The specified undertaking of Unit Trust of India, functioning under an administrator and under the rules framed by Government of India and does not come under the purview of the mutual fund regulations. It has US-64 and the assured returns schemes. The second is the UTI Mutual Fund Ltd., sponsored by State Bank of India (SBI), Bank of Baroda (BoB), Punjab National Bank (PNB) and Life Insurance Corporation (LIC) of India. It is registered with SEBI and functions under the mutual fund regulations. It is an unencumbered mutual fund, with only NAV-based schemes.

The problem with US-64 scheme of UTI adversely affected the resource mobilisation by mutual funds in general and UTI in particular. On both the occasions, when UTI faced difficulties and while resource mobilisation by UTI declined sharply, private sector mutual funds were able to fill the gap created by UTI only partially as overall mobilisation by all mutual funds on both the occasions declined sharply after the occurrence of the problem.

In March 2002, guidelines were issued to enable mutual funds to invest in rated securities in countries with fully convertible currencies. This marked an important milestone, through which mutual funds will be able to deliver better risk/return tradeoffs through international diversification.

Features of Mutual Fund Industry in India: Mutual funds are popular mainly with the middle and high-income groups.

1. Investors are largely based in the urban centres, particularly the metropolitan cities.
2. Penetration of mutual funds in the rural areas remains small.
3. UTI and other state-owned asset management companies have lost market share, while private sector funds have grown rapidly.
4. Asset management companies are divided into those that are predominantly owned by the state (UTI, bank sponsored and institutions) and those that are in the private sector.
5. Mutual fund industry has to compete with attractive assured returns from Government schemes and this is possibly the single most important impediment to the growth of the industry.

Thus, if mutual funds have to grow fast, they would need to devise appropriate schemes to attract the saving of low-income groups, especially in rural areas. This is the only way to ensure participation of all categories of investors into the capital market, which is so crucial for its long-term development.

Problems of Mutual Funds: India has a high household savings ratio. Indians, like most people anywhere, are conservative in their habits, and it would take many years to change this behaviour, particularly when it comes to the use of their savings. As in most countries, investment in physical assets (mainly housing and gold) accounts for the most important percentage of household assets. Owning a home is usually a first priority once a family has any disposable income at all.

Competition with Government Schemes: Mutual funds compete against a host of high yielding government-backed savings schemes such as public provident fund (PPF), National Savings Scheme (NSS), RBI Bonds, and so on, as well as against life insurance products and, in the future, against the new pension schemes for the unorganised sector. The political and social reasons for keeping yields higher than the market for small savers, particularly retired savers, is understandable. The market is distorted by such a policy. Government should have the strategic aim of discontinuing over time or at least reducing the availability of the unrealistically high yielding avenues for small savings. The objective of widening and deepening ownership of mutual funds is unlikely to be met until this happens.

Fixed income and balanced mutual funds have offered a reasonably competitive rate of return but they are not guaranteed, a key attraction to Indian investors. The net result is that mutual funds fail to attract much money from retail investors, who prefer to invest in a no-risk, high return product, i.e. government saving schemes or provident funds or keep their money safely in the bank.

Government-sponsored instruments *crowd out* mutual funds since for the majority of Indians buying mutual funds, before they have their full complement of government-backed savings instruments, would be both wrong and foolish.

In most countries, government guaranteed financial instruments offer returns that are likely to be significantly lower than private sector investments available from mutual funds or insurance companies. This is the penalty that investors are prepared to pay for little or no risk. However, Indian retail investors are not being asked to sacrifice any substantial amount of return in exchange for a government guarantee. Conversely, returns on government assured investments are often better than those available elsewhere. While conventional government bonds do give lower returns than equivalent private sector corporate bonds, the retail government assured products give higher returns for almost no risk. It is thus hardly surprising that an investor of modest means would choose to invest in, for instance, national savings certificates, since he can thus obtain a better return for a much lower risk. Any investor would be well advised to invest the maximum permitted in the various government assured schemes before considering other forms of investment.

The reasons why the government is prepared to pay above market rates of interest on certain financial products is understandable. At a time when interest rates have fallen substantially from their previous levels, savers who had counted on the interest on their savings to provide an income, particularly in retirement, are being subsidised. Given that pension arrangements, particularly in the unorganised sector, are not widespread, such an approach is reasonable and indeed most small savers are acting rationally when they choose the low risk option. However, this approach conflicts with a desire to widen and deepen participation in capital markets through mutual funds or other non-governmental savings products by the less well-off sectors of the population.

Competition from Insurance: The take up life assurance is growing rapidly and may be pre-empting some of the market that mutual funds could aim at. Life assurance is an easier product to sell, since in the mind of the investor the payment of a premium is often linked to a specific outcome, a lump sum payment on death or a guaranteed minimum sum on maturity. It also pays higher commissions to sales agents (typically the amount of the first 5 to 6 months premium). Thus, a sales agent will usually prefer to sell a life policy since it will reward him better.

Volatility of Mutual Fund Performance: There is a perception that mutual funds have somehow let down their investors and given them poor returns. In July 2001 when UTI slashed down the dividend rates for the year 2000-01 and suspended sales and repurchases of US-64 for a period of 6 months from July 2001 to December 2001, it created a crisis of confidence among the investors with long-term effects.

Tax System Encourages Short-term Objectives: Mutual funds are regarded in most countries as a diversified, professionally managed and well-regulated vehicle for mobilising household savings and are often accorded tax privileges specifically in pursuit of a government policy goal to encourage long-term savings, notably for retirement. It is unusual for such tax privileges to impel mutual funds towards short-term goals, which is what seems to be the case in India. True, Indian unit trusts are diversified, professionally managed and well-regulated, but they are certainly not serving long-term objectives.

Mutual Funds and the Stock Market: Mutual funds in India, because of their small size and slower growth in the recent past, have tended to play only a limited role in the stock market. In view of small size of their operations, mutual funds in normal times hardly exert any influence on the stock market. Nonetheless, major developments concerning mutual funds do exert significant influence on the sentiment. The negative developments at UTI such as reporting of negative corpus for US-64 in October 1998, heavy redemption pressure on US-64 units in July 2001 etc. resulted in decline in the BSE Sensex. On the other hand, positive developments like implementation of special unit scheme and announcement of positive corpus for US-64 were associated with general uptrend in the equity prices.

Mutual funds with large funds at their disposal are expected by the government to act as a counterweight to foreign institutional investors (FIIs), which generally exert a significant influence on the stock market.

The mutual fund industry in India is quite sophisticated and successful. It is dominated by good and reputable institutions, both Indian and international. Nevertheless improvements are always possible and desirable in order to enhance the ability of the mutual fund industry to mobilise savings on a wider scale and to contribute to the further development of capital market.

Although reforms in the financial sector since 1991 have been successful in creating a competitive environment, the growth of mutual funds has slowed down, partly due to the problems faced by UTI.

Nn

NASDAQ: See National Association of Securities Dealers Automated Quotations, *143*.

National Association of Securities Dealers Automated Quotations (NASDAQ): It is the largest US electronic stock market. This is an organization that does exactly what its name stands for. The system provides a computerized information network through which brokers, banks and other investment professionals can obtain up-to-the-minute price quotations on securities traded over the counter.

National Electronic Funds Transfer (NEFT): The NEFT was launched by the RBI in November 2005 as a more secure, nation-wide retail electronic payment system to facilitate funds transfer by the bank customers, between the networked bank branches in the country. It has, however, been observed that the public sector banks are not the most active users of this product and the majority of NEFT outward transactions are originated by a few new-generation private sector banks and foreign banks.

In order to popularise the e-payments in the country, the RBI, on its part, waived the service charges to be levied on the member banks, till March 31, 2009, in respect of the Real Time Gross Settlement (RTGS) and NEFT transactions. The RBI also provides, free of charge, intra-day liquidity to the banks for the RTGS transactions. The service charges to be levied by banks from their customers for RTGS and NEFT have, however, been deregulated and left to the discretion of the individual banks. While some of the banks have rationalised their service charges and a few have made it even cost-free to the customers, there are also certain banks that have fixed unreasonably high service charges for providing these services to their customers—even though the RBI provides these services to the banks free of charge.

National Exchange for Automated Trading (NEAT-F&O): Futures and options trading system of NSE— called NEAT-F&O trading system—provides a fully automated screen-based trading for index futures and options, stock futures and options and futures on interest rate on a nationwide basis as well as an online monitoring and surveillance mechanism. It supports an order driven market and provides complete transparency of trading operations. It is similar to that of trading of equities in the cash market segment.

The software for the F&O market has been developed to facilitate efficient and transparent trading in futures and options instruments. Keeping in view the familiarity of trading members with the current capital market trading system, modifications have been introduced in the existing capital market trading system so as to make it suitable for trading futures and options.

Trading Mechanism: The NEAT-F&O system supports an order driven market, wherein orders match automatically. Order matching is essentially on the basis of security, its price, time and quantity. All quantity fields are in units and price in rupees. The lot size on the futures and options market is 50 for Nifty. The exchange notifies the regular lot size and tick size for each security traded on this segment from time to time. Orders, as and when they are received, are first time stamped and then immediately processed for potential match. When any order enters the trading system, it is an active order. If it finds a match, a trade is generated. If a match is not found, then the orders are stored in different *books*. Orders are stored in price-time priority in various books in the following sequence: (a) best price, and (b) within price, by time priority.

Entities in the Trading System: There are four entities in the trading system:

1. **Trading Members:** Trading members are members of NSE. They can trade either on their own account or on behalf of their clients including participants. The exchange assigns ID to each trading member. Each trading member can have more than one user.

2. **Clearing Members:** Clearing members are members of NSCCL. They carry out risk management activities and confirmation/inquiry of trades through the trading system.
3. **Professional Clearing Members:** Professional clearing members are clearing members who are not trading member. Typically, banks and custodians become professional clearing members and clear and settle for their trading members.
4. **Participants:** A participant is a client of trading members like financial institutions. These clients may trade through multiple trading members but settle through a single clearing member.

Corporate Hierarchy: In the F&O trading software, a trading member has the facility of defining a hierarchy amongst users of the system. This hierarchy comprises corporate manager, branch manager and dealer.

1. **Corporate Manager:** The term *corporate manager* is assigned to a user placed at the highest level in a trading firm. Such a user can perform all the functions such as order and trade-related activities, receiving reports for all branches of the trading member firm and also all dealers of the firm. Additionally, a corporate manager can define exposure limits for the branches of the firm. This facility is available only to the corporate manager.
2. **Branch Manager:** The branch manager is a term assigned to a user who is placed under the corporate manager. Such a user can perform and view order and trade-related activities for all dealers under that branch.
3. **Dealer:** Dealer is a user at the lower level of the hierarchy. A dealer can perform trade-related activities only for himself and does not have access to information on other dealers under either the same branch or other branches.

National Securities Clearing Corporation Ltd. (NSCCL): NSCCL, a wholly-owned subsidiary of NSE, was incorporated in August 1995 and commenced operating as a clearing corporation in April 1996. Clearing and settlement operations of the NSE are managed by NSCCL. It was the first clearing corporation to provide novation/settlement guarantee that revolutionised the entire concept of settlement system in India. It was set up to: (a) bring and sustain confidence in clearing and settlement of securities, (b) promote and maintain short and consistent settlement cycles, (c) provide counterparty risk guarantee, and (d) operate a tight risk containment system.

NSCCL undertakes clearing of transactions executed on the National Stock Exchange for Automated Trading (NEAT) system of NSE. It carries out clearing and settlement functions as per the settlement cycles of different sub-segments in the equities segment. The reforms in the securities settlement systems have resulted in following benefits:

1. Reduction and mitigation of systemic, structural and operational risks.
2. Increase speed of transaction, execution and settlement of trade and quicker settlement of transactions with finality.
3. Safety of the settlement process.
4. Reduction of transaction costs and, thereby, making market more efficient and transparent for investors and participants. See also Bank of India Shareholding Ltd. (BOISL).

National Securities Depository Limited (NSDL): It was created in 1995. Based in Mumbai, it was the first central securities depository in India. Promoted by institutions of national stature responsible for the economic development of India, it has established a national infrastructure of international standards that handles most of the securities held and settled in dematerialised form in the Indian capital market.

Although India had a vibrant capital market which is more than a century old, the paper-based settlement of trades caused substantial problems such as bad delivery and delayed transfer of title. The enactment of Depositories Act in August 1996 paved the way for establishment of NSDL, the first depository in India. It went on to establish infrastructure based on international standards.

NSDL has the objective of ensuring the safety and soundness of Indian marketplaces by developing settlement solutions that increase efficiency, minimise risk and reduce costs. NSDL plays a quiet but central role in developing products and services that will continue to nurture the growing needs of the financial services industry.

In the depository system, securities are held in depository accounts, which are similar to holding funds in bank accounts. Transfer of ownership of securities is done through simple account transfers. This method does away with all the risks and hassles normally associated with paperwork. Consequently, the cost of transacting in a depository environment is considerably lower as compared to transacting in certificates.

NSDL is promoted by Industrial Development Bank of India Limited (IDBI)—the largest development bank of India, Unit Trust of India (UTI)—the largest mutual fund in India and National Stock Exchange of India Limited (NSE)—the largest stock exchange in India. Some of the prominent banks in the country have taken a stake in NSDL.

National Stock Exchange of India Limited (NSE): It is located in Mumbai, India. NSE was established in the mid-1990s as a demutualised electronic exchange. NSE provides a modern, fully automated screen-based trading system, with over two lakh trading terminals, through which investors in every nook and corner of India can trade. NSE has played a critical role in reforming the Indian securities market and in bringing unparalleled transparency, efficiency and market integrity.

Though a number of other exchanges exist, NSE and the Bombay Stock Exchange (BSE) are the two most significant stock exchanges in India, and between them are responsible for the vast majority of share transactions. NSE's flagship index, the CNX NIFTY 50, is used extensively by investors in India and around the world to take exposure to the Indian equities market.

NSE was started by a clutch of leading Indian financial institutions. It offers trading, clearing and settlement services in equity, debt and equity derivatives. It is India's largest exchange, globally in cash market trades, in currency trading and index options. NSE has diversified shareholding. There are many domestic and global institutions and companies that hold stake in the exchange.

NSC was incorporated in 1992 and recognised as a stock exchange in 1993, at a time when P.V. Narasimha Rao was the Prime Minister of India and Dr. Manmohan Singh was the Finance Minister. It was set up to bring in transparency in the markets. Promoted by leading financial institutions, essentially led by IDBI at the behest of the Government of India, it was incorporated in November 1992 as a tax-paying company. In April 1993, it was recognised as a stock exchange under the Securities Contracts (Regulation) Act, 1956. NSE commenced operations in the Wholesale Debt Market (WDM) segment in June 1994. The Capital market (Equities) segment of the NSE commenced operations in November 1994, while operations in the Derivatives segment commenced in June 2000.

NSE changed the way the Indian markets functioned, in the early 1990s, by replacing floor-based trading with nationwide screen-based electronic trading, which took trading to the doorstep of the investor. The exchange was mainly set up to bring in transparency in the markets. Instead of trading membership being confined to a group of brokers, the NSE ensured that anyone who was qualified, experienced and met minimum financial requirements was allowed to trade.

In this context, the NSE was ahead of its times, when it separated ownership and management in the exchange under SEBI's supervision. The price information which could earlier be accessed only by a handful of people can now be seen by a client in a remote location with the same ease. The paper-based settlement has been replaced by electronic depository-based accounts and settlement of trades. A robust risk management system is in place, so that settlement guarantees could protect investors against broker defaults.

NSE was also instrumental in creating the National Securities

Depository Limited (NSDL) which allows investors to securely hold and transfer their shares and bonds electronically. It also allows investors to hold and trade in as few as one share or bond. This not only makes holding financial instruments convenient, but more importantly eliminates the need for paper certificates and greatly reduces the incidents of forged or fake certificates and fraudulent transactions that had plagued the Indian stock market. NSDL's security, combined with the transparency, lower transaction prices and efficiency that the NSE offers, has greatly increased the attractiveness of the Indian stock market to domestic and international investors.

Currently, NSE has the following major segments of the capital market:

Equities:

- Equities.
- Indices.
- Mutual funds.
- Exchange traded funds.
- Initial public offerings.
- Security lending and borrowing scheme.

Derivatives

- Equity derivatives (including global indices like S&P 500, Dow Jones and FTSE).
- Currency derivatives.
- Interest rate futures.

Debt

- Corporate bonds.

Equity Derivatives: NSE commenced trading in derivatives with the launch of index futures on June 12, 2000. The futures and options segment of NSE has made a mark for itself globally. In the Futures and Options segment, trading in CNX Nifty Index, CNX IT Index, Bank Nifty Index, Nifty Midcap 50 index and single stock futures are available. Trading in Mini Nifty Futures and Options and Long-term Options on CNX Nifty are also available.

On August 29, 2011, NSE launched derivative contracts on

the world's most followed equity indices, the S&P 500 and the Dow Jones Industrial Average. NSE is the first Indian exchange to launch global indices. This is also the first time in the world that futures contracts on the S&P 500 index were introduced and listed on an exchange outside of their home country, USA. The new contracts include futures on both the DJIA and the S&P 500, and options on the S&P 500.

On May 3, 2012, NSE launched derivative contracts (futures and options) on FTSE 100, the widely tracked index of the UK equity stock market. This was the first of its kind of an index of the UK equity stock market launched in India. FTSE 100 includes 100 largest UK listed blue chip companies.

On January 10, 2013, NSE signed a letter of intent with the Japan Exchange Group, Inc. (JPX) on preparing for the launch of CNX Nifty Index futures, a representative stock price index of India, on the Osaka Securities Exchange Co., Ltd. (OSE), a subsidiary of JPX. Moving forward, both parties will make preparations for the listing of yen-denominated CNX Nifty Index futures by March 2014. Retail and institutional investors in Japan will be able to take a view on the Indian markets in their own currency and in their own time zone. Investors will therefore not face any currency risk, because they will not have to invest in dollar denominated or rupee denominated contracts.

Currency Derivatives: In August 2008, currency derivatives were introduced in India by NSE with the launch of currency futures in US$ and INR. It also added currency futures in Euros, Pounds and Yen.

Interest Rate Futures: Interest rate futures were introduced for the first time in India by NSE on August 31, 2009, exactly one year after the launch of currency futures. NSE became the first stock exchange to get an approval for interest rate futures, as recommended by the SEBI-RBI committee.

Debt Market: On May 13, 2013, NSE launched India's first dedicated debt platform to provide a liquid and transparent trading platform for debt related products. The debt segment provides an opportunity to retail investors to invest in corporate bonds on a liquid and transparent exchange platform. It also helps institutions who are holders of corporate bonds. It is an ideal platform to buy and sell at optimum prices and help corporates to get adequate demand, when they are issuing the bonds.

Financial Literacy: NSE is keen to ensure that the people of India are empowered to take sound financial decisions and invest wisely. It has collaborated, among others, with several universities like Gokhale Institute of Politics and Economics, Pune; Bharati Vidyapeeth Deemed University, Pune; Guru Gobind Singh Indraprastha University, Delhi; Ravenshaw University of Cuttack and Punjabi University, Patiala, to offer MBA and BBA courses. NSE has also provided mock market simulation software called NSE Learn to Trade (NLT) to develop investment, trading and portfolio management skills among the students. The simulation software is very similar to the software currently being used by the market professionals and helps students to learn how to trade in the markets.

The exchange has also worked with a missionary zeal to educate investors about the opportunities in the market, the precautions they should take and their rights and obligations. In order to educate investors and help them invest wisely, NSE conducts nearly 1,500 seminars every year in the metros as well as the smallest towns of India.

NSE also conducts online examination and awards certification, under its Certification in Financial Markets (NCFM) programmes. At present, certifications are available in 46 modules, covering different sectors of financial and capital markets, both at the beginner and advanced levels. The list of various modules can be found at the official site of NSE India. In addition, since August 2009, it offers a short-term course called NSE Certified Capital Market Professional (NCCMP). The NCCMP is a 100 hour programme for over 3-4 months, conducted at the colleges, and covers theoretical and practical training in subjects related to the capital markets. NCCMP covers subjects like equity markets, debt markets, derivatives, macroeconomics, technical analysis and fundamental analysis. Successful candidates are awarded joint certification from NSE and the concerned college. See also Bombay Stock Exchange (BSE).

Negotiated Dealing System (NDS): It is an electronic platform for facilitating dealing in Government securities and money market instruments, introduced by RBI.

Net Asset Value (NAV): It is the current market worth of a mutual fund's share. A fund's net asset value is calculated by taking the fund's total assets, securities, cash and any accrued earnings, deducting liabilities, and dividing the remainder by the number of units outstanding.

Net Dividend: Dividend after deduction of tax payable from gross dividend.

Net Liquid Assets: Cash and readily marketable securities minus current liabilities of a company. This is the strictest test of a company's ability to meet current debt obligations.

Net Position: The difference between the buy and sell contracts held by a trader.

Net Worth: The aggregate value of the paid up equity capital and free reserves (excluding reserves created out of revaluation), reduced by the aggregate value of accumulated losses and deferred expenditure not written off, including miscellaneous expenses not written of.

New Issue: Shares of a company offered to the public, through a public issue, for the first time to be listed on the Stock Exchange.

New York Stock Exchange (NYSE): It is the world's leading equities market with world-class companies listed on it.

Non-banking Financial Companies (NBFCs): In the multi-tier financial system of India, NBFCs stand apart for more than one reason. Though these companies essentially do the job of financial intermediation, they are still not fully comparable with the other segments of the financial system. This is so in view of the wide variations in the profile of the players in this sector in terms of their nature of activity—lending, investment, lease, hire purchase, chit fund, pure deposit mobilisation, fee based activity etc. —the volume of activity, the sources of funding they rely on (public deposits and non-public deposits), method of raising resources, deployment pattern etc. This has naturally resulted in the creation of multifarious categories of NBFCs and therefore, diverse regulatory dispensation by RBI.

Classification of NBFCs: NBFCs comprise a heterogeneous lot of privately-owned, small-sized financial intermediaries which provide a variety of services including equipment leasing, hire purchase, loans, investments and chit fund activities. These companies play an important role in providing credit to the unorganised sector and to the small borrowers at the local level. Hire purchase finance is by far the largest activity of NBFCs.

Though heterogeneous, NBFCs can be broadly classified into three categories: (a) asset finance companies (such as equipment leasing and hire purchase), (b) loan companies, and (c) investment companies.

A separate category of NBFCs, called the residuary non-banking companies (RNBCs), also exists as it has not been categorised into any one of the above referred three categories.

Besides, there are miscellaneous non-banking companies (chit funds), mutual benefit financial companies (*Nidhis* and unnotified *Nidhis*) and housing finance companies.

In terms of regulation and supervision, there are two broad categories of Non-banking Financial Companies (NBFCs), viz. Non-banking Financial Companies–Deposit Taking (NBFCs-D) and Non-banking Financial Companies–Non-deposit Taking (NBFCs-ND). While NBFCs-D have been regulated by the RBI from 1963, an amendment to the RBI Act in 1997 empowered the RBI to regulate and supervise all categories of NBFCs more comprehensively. NBFCs-ND, until recently, were subject to minimal regulation as they were non-deposit taking. Recognising, however, the growing importance of this segment and their linkages to banks and other financial institutions, capital adequacy and exposure norms were made applicable to NBFCs-ND with assets above ₹ 100 crore from April 1, 2007.

The role of NBFCs in transferring the funds from lenders to borrowers has been well-recognized. The main advantages of these companies are as under:

1. Customer orientation and prompt provision of services.
2. Concentration in the main financial centres.
3. Attractive rates of return offered.
4. Lower transactions costs of operations.
5. Quick decision-making ability.
6. Simplified sanction procedures.
7. Flexibility and timeliness in meeting the credit needs of specified sectors (like equipment leasing and hire purchase).

On account of these advantages, NBFCs have in recent years grown sizeably both in terms of their numbers as well as the volume of business transactions.

NBFCs have been the subject of focussed attention since the early 1990s. The rapid growth of NBFCs has led to a gradual blurring of dividing lines between banks and NBFCs, with the exception of the exclusive privilege that commercial banks exercise in the issuance of cheques.

NBFCs are widely dispersed across the country and their management exhibits varied degrees of professionalism. Furthermore, the depositors have varied degrees of perceptions regarding safety of their deposits while making an investment decision.

In June 2000, NBFCs registered with the RBI were permitted, with prior approval of the RBI, to set up insurance joint ventures for undertaking insurance business with risk participation. Similarly, NBFCs registered with the RBI that have net owned funds of ₹ 5 crore and more are permitted to undertake insurance business as agent of insurance companies on a fee basis, without any risk participation. A minimum 12 percent capital adequacy for NBFCs which want to enter into insurance joint ventures has been prescribed. If the company holds public deposits, the minimum capital adequacy has been proposed at 15 percent. Further, minimum net worth requirement of ₹ 500 crore, three years of continuous net profit, and maximum non-performing assets of 5 percent of the total outstanding leased/hire purchase assets and advances have been prescribed for NBFCs.

In February 2004, it was decided to allow NBFCs registered with the RBI to take up insurance agency business on a fee basis and without risk participation, without the approval of the RBI subject to certain conditions.

Non-performing Asset (NPA): An asset, including a leased asset, becomes non-performing when it ceases to generate income for the bank.

Non-resident Indian (NRI): An Indian citizen who stays abroad for employment/carrying on business or stays abroad under circumstances indicating an intention for an uncertain duration of stay abroad.

Non-voting Stocks: These are shares that do not give voting rights to the holder. The category includes participating preference shares.

NYSE: See New York Stock Exchange, *152*.

Oo

Odd Lot: See Marketable Lot, *127*.

Offer: Willingness to sell a contract at a given price.

Offer Price: Price at which units in trust can be bought. It often includes an entry fee. It also refers to the price at which securities are offered to the public.

Ombudsman: An independent person appointed to hear and act upon citizens' complaints about government services. Invented in Sweden, the idea has been widely adopted. For example, groups of banks, mortgage lenders and insurance companies in various countries have appointed ombudsmen to attend to the complaints of their customers. Customers who use the ombudsman's (free) service retain their full right to take legal action should they not agree with the ombudsman's decision.

Open Market Operations: See Reserve Bank of India, *184*.

Open Order: An order to buy and sell a security that remains in effect until it is either cancelled by the customer or executed.

Open-ended Scheme: An open-ended fund or scheme is one that is available for subscription and repurchase on a continuous basis.

Opening Price: The rate at which the first transaction in a security is struck after the opening of the market.

Operational Risk: The risk that deficiencies in information systems or internal controls could result in unexpected losses.

The revised BASEL II framework offers the following three approaches for estimating capital charges for operational risk.

Basic Indicator Approach (BIA): This approach sets a

charge for operational risk as a fixed percentage (*alpha factor*) of a single indicator, which serves as a proxy for the bank's risk exposure.

Standardised Approach (SA): This approach requires that the institution separate its operations into eight standard business lines, and the capital charge for each business line is calculated by multiplying gross income of that business line by a factor (denoted beta) assigned to that business line.

Advanced Measurement Approach (AMA): Under this approach, the regulatory capital requirement will equal the risk measure generated by the banks' internal operational risk measurement system.

In India, the banks have been advised to adopt the BIA to estimate the capital charge for operational risk and 15 percent of average gross income of last three years is taken for calculating capital charge for operational risk.

Option Holder: The person who buys the option contract is known as the holder of an option. In purchasing the option, the buyer makes payments and receives rights to buy or sell the underlying on specific terms.

Option Premium: The premium is the price at which the contract trades. The premium is the price of the option and is paid by the buyer to the writer or seller of the option. In return, the writer of a call option is obligated to deliver the underlying security to an option buyer if the call is exercised or buy the underlying security if the put is exercised. The writer keeps the premium whether or not the option is exercised.

Option Price: Option price is the price that the option buyer pays to the option seller. It is also referred to as the option premium.

Option Seller: Also called the option writer, it is the party who grants a right to trade a security at a given price in the future.

Option Spread: A spread is a type of option position where you buy an option and sell an option and both of them are from the same option class.

Options: An option is a contract which gives the buyer the right, but not the obligation, to buy or sell specified quantity of the underlying assets, at a specific (strike) price on or before a specified time (expiration date). The underlying may be a commodity like wheat or rice or financial instrument like equity stock or bonds etc. Options are basically of two types: call options and put options.

Call Options: A call option is an option to buy a stock at a specific price on or before a certain date. In this way, call options are like security deposits. If, for example, Mr. Wilson wants to rent a certain property, and leaves a security deposit for it, the money would be used to insure that he would, in fact, rent that property at the price agreed upon when he returns. If Mr. Wilson never returns, he would lose his security deposit, but he would have no other liability.

Call options usually increase in value as the value of the underlying instrument rises. When you buy a call option, the price you pay for it, called the option premium, secures your right to buy that certain stock at a specified price called the strike price. If you decide not to use the option to buy the stock, and you are not obligated to, your only cost is the *option premium*.

Put Options: Put options are options to sell a stock at a specific price on or before a certain date. In this way, put options are like insurance policies. If you buy a new car, and then buy auto insurance on the car, you pay a premium and are, hence, protected if the asset is damaged in an accident. If this happens, you can use your policy to regain the insured value of the car. In this way, the put option gains in value as the value of the underlying instrument decreases. If all goes well and the insurance is not needed, the insurance company keeps your premium in return for taking on the risk.

With a put option, you can *insure* a stock by fixing a selling price. If something happens which causes the stock price to fall, and thus, *damages* your asset, you can exercise your option and sell it at its *insured* price level. If the price of your stock goes up, and there is no *damage*, then you do not need to use the insurance, and, once again, your only cost is the premium.

Buying put options is buying insurance. To buy a put option on Nifty is to buy insurance which reimburses the full extent to which Nifty drops below the strike price of the put option. This is attractive to many people, and to mutual funds creating *guaranteed return products*. The Nifty index fund industry will find it very useful to make a bundle of a Nifty index fund and a Nifty put option to create a new kind of a Nifty index fund, which gives the investor protection against extreme drops in Nifty. Selling put options is selling insurance, so anyone who feels like earning revenues by selling insurance can set himself up to do so on the index options market.

Like forwards and futures, options represent another derivative instrument and provide a mechanism by which one can acquire a certain commodity or other asset in order to make profit or cover risk for a price. The options are similar to the future contracts in the sense that they are also standardized but are different from them in many ways. Options, in fact, represent the rights.

An option is the right, but not the obligation, to buy or sell a specified amount (and quality) of a commodity, currency, index, or financial instrument, or to buy or sell a specified number of underlying future contracts, at a specific price on or before a given date in future. Like other contracts, there are two parties to an option contract: the buyer who takes a long position and the seller or writer, who takes a short position. The option contract gives the owner a right to buy/sell a particular commodity or other asset at a specific pre-destined price by a specified date. The price involved is called exercise or strike price and the date involved is known as expiration. It is important to understand that such a contract gives its holder the right, and not the obligation to buy/sell. The option writer, on the other hand, undertakes upon himself the obligation to sell/buy the underlying asset if that suits the option holder. There is a wide variety of underlying assets including agricultural commodities, metals, shares, indices and so on, on which options are written.

Further, like future contracts, options are also tradable on exchanges. The exchange-traded options are standardized contracts and their trading is regulated by the exchanges that ensure the honouring of such contracts. Thus, in case of options as well, a clearing corporation takes the other side in every contract so that the party with the long position has a claim against the clearing corporation and the one with short position is obliged to it. However, buying or selling of future contracts does not require any price to be paid, called premium. The writer of an option receives the premium as a compensation of the risk that he takes upon himself. The premium belongs to the writer and is not adjusted in the price if the holder of the option decides to exercise it. This price is determined on the exchange, like the price of a share, by the forces of demand and supply. Further, like the share prices, the option prices also keep on changing with passage of time as trading takes place.

One difference between future and option trading may be noted. Whereas both parties to a future contract are required to deposit margins to the exchange, only the party with the short position is called upon to pay margin in case of options trading. The party with the long position does not pay anything beyond the premium.

Advantages of Option Trading: These are as under:

Risk Management: Put options allow investors holding shares to hedge against a possible fall in their value. This can be considered similar to taking out insurance against a fall in the share price.

Time to Decide: By taking a call option the purchase price for the shares is locked-in. This gives the call option holder until the expiry day to decide whether or not to exercise the option and buy the shares. Likewise, the taker of a put option has time to decide whether or not to sell the shares.

Speculation: The ease of trading in and out of an option position makes it possible to trade options with no intention of ever exercising them. If an investor expects the market to rise, he may decide to buy call options. If expecting a fall, he may decide to buy put options. Either way the holder can sell the option prior to expiry to take a profit or limit a loss. Trading options has a lower cost than shares, as there is no stamp duty payable unless and until options are exercised.

Leverage: Leverage provides the potential to make a higher return from a smaller initial outlay than investing directly. However, leverage usually involves more risks than a direct investment in the underlying shares. Trading in options can allow investors to benefit from a change in the price of the share without having to pay the full price of the share.

Income Generation: Shareholders can earn extra income over and above dividends by writing call options against their shares. By writing an option they receive the option premium upfront. While they get to keep the option premium, there is a possibility that they could be exercised against and have to deliver their shares to the taker at the exercise price.

Strategies: By combining different options, investors can create a wide range of potential profit scenarios.

Distinction between Futures and Options: Options are different from futures in several respects. At a practical level, the option buyer pays for the option in full at the time it is purchased. After this, he only has an upside. There is no possibility of the options position generating any further loss to him—other than the funds already paid for the option. Contrarily, futures are free to enter into but can generate very large losses. This feature makes options attractive to many occasional market participants who do not have time to monitor their futures positions.

More generally, options offer *non-linear payoffs* whereas futures only have *linear payoffs*. By combining futures and options, a wide variety of innovative and useful payoff structures can be created.

Pricing Options: Black-Scholes Formulae: An option buyer has the right but not the obligation to exercise on the seller. The worst that can happen to a buyer is the loss of the premium paid by him. His downside is limited to this premium, but his upside is potentially unlimited. This optionality is precious and has a value, which is expressed in terms of the option price. Just like in other free markets, it is the supply and demand in the secondary market that drives the price of an option.

There are various models which help us get close to the true price of an option. Most of these are variants of the celebrated Black-Scholes model for pricing European options. Today most calculators and spread-sheets come with a built-in Black-Scholes options pricing formula so to price options we do not really need to memorise the formula.

Options have existed—at least in concept—since antiquity. It was not until publication of the Black-Scholes (1973) option pricing formula that a theoretically consistent framework for pricing options became available. That framework was a direct result of work by Robert Merton as well as Fisher Black and Myron Scholes. In 1997, Scholes and Merton won the Nobel Prize in economics for this work. Black had died in 1995, but otherwise would have shared the prize.

The factors affecting the option price are the following:

1. Spot price of the underlying.
2. Exercise price.
3. Risk-free interest rate.
4. Volatility of the underlying.
5. Time to expiration.
6. Dividends on the underlying (stock or index).

Interestingly, before Black and Scholes came up with their option pricing model, there was a widespread belief that the expected growth of the underlying ought to affect the option price. Black and Scholes demonstrate that this is not true. The significance of the Black and Scholes model is that like any good model, it tells us what is important and what is not. It does not promise to produce the exact prices that show up in the market, but certainly does a remarkable job of pricing options within the framework of assumptions of the model. Virtually all option pricing models, even the most complex ones, have much in common with the Black-Scholes model.

Black and Scholes start by specifying a simple and well-known equation that models the way in which stock prices fluctuate. This equation called Geometric Brownian Motion, implies that stock returns will have a lognormal distribution, meaning that the logarithm of the stock's return will follow the normal (bell-shaped) distribution. Black and Scholes then propose that the option's price is determined by only two variables that are allowed to change: time and the underlying stock price. The other factors, namely the volatility, the exercise price, and the risk-free interest rate do affect the option's price but they are not allowed to change. By forming a portfolio consisting of a long position in stock and a short position in calls, the risk of the stock is eliminated. This hedged portfolio is obtained by setting the number of shares of stock equal to the approximate change in the call price for a change in the stock price. This mix of stock and calls must be revised continuously, a process known as delta hedging.

Black and Scholes then turn to a little-known result in a specialised field of probability known as stochastic calculus. This result defines how the option price changes in terms of the change in the stock price and time to expiration. They then reason that this hedged combination of options and stock should grow in value at the risk-free rate. The result then is a partial differential equation. The solution is found by forcing a condition called a boundary condition on the model that requires the option price to converge to the exercise value at expiration. The end result is the Black and Scholes model.

Order Book: It is an *electronic book* that shows the demand for the shares of the company at various prices.

Orders (Types): In the stock market, when prices of the well-traded securities are quoted, full prices are seldom indicated. The system allows the trading members to enter orders with various conditions attached to them as per their requirements. The various kinds of order given by various traders are explained below.

Market Order: Market order is the most common type of order and simply involves an instruction to buy or sell at the prevailing price in the market. It represents the best price one can get at a point of time. Small orders can be conveniently executed at the market rate but if the size of the order is larger than the volume which is currently available in the dealing pit, then executions might not all be at the same price because the dealer would have to bid up or offer down until desired volumes are secured. Thus, large orders *at market* have a tendency to move against those who give them. No wonder then that large orders may be placed by market participants who wish to move the market in a particular direction.

Limit Order: A limit order is an order to buy or sell at a specified price, or a price better than that. Thus, a limit order is exemplified when a client may give a broker a price limit above which he should not buy or below which he should not sell. Also, there is a time limit for which it may be given. This kind of an order puts more responsibility on the dealer since he has to be aware of his limits orders once the limit is reached. A limit order kind of order is feasible when it is considered that there is sufficient market force in the opposite direction at current prices. This has the advantage that it is far less likely to push prices in an adverse direction.

Stop-Loss Order: A stop-loss order is aimed at closing out positions when a particular price level is traded. It is this kind of an order when a client orders his broker to sell a share or some other security, if its market price falls to a certain level below the current price. Thus, once the specified price is reached or penetrated, the order becomes the market order. Stop-loss orders are a good means of protecting profits or limiting losses while waiting for the market to recover.

Stop-Limit Order: A stop-limit order is said to be placed when, for example, a client can place a stop order at a particular level with a limit beyond which the market would cease to be chased.

Fill or Kill Order: This is an order to a broker to buy or sell a security or derivative immediately. If the order is not executed at once, it is treated as withdrawn. This type of an order is often used by a party wishing to take out a large bid/offer but, in case of a failure, it does not wish to be viewed as a possible large counter party in the market.

Market if Touched (MIT): It is a limit order which automatically becomes a market order once a predetermined price is reached.

Good Till Cancelled (GTC): This is a client's order to buy or sell, usually at a specified price, which remains valid until its execution or cancellation.

Day Order or Good for the Day: As the name implies, this means the limits or stop order would lapse at the end of the day (of dealing) if it has not been executed during the day.

Ordinary Shares: Ordinary shares represent ownership capital and their owners—ordinary shareholders—share the reward and risk associated with ownership of corporate enterprises. They are called ordinary shares in contrast with preference shares which carry certain prior rights with regard to income and redemption.

There are certain concepts associated with ordinary shares. Authorised equity represents the maximum amount that a company can raise from the ordinary shareholders. It can be changed in the prescribed manner. The portion of the authorized capital offered by the company to investors is the issued capital. Subscribed share capital is that part of the issued capital which has been subscribed by the investors. The actual amount paid by the shareholders is the paid-up capital. The issued, subscribed and paid-up capitals are generally the same.

Ordinary shares typically have a face value in terms of the price of each share, the most popular denomination being ₹ 10. However, companies are permitted to issue such shares without a face value. The price at which the ordinary shares are issued is the issue price. The issue price for new companies is generally equal to the face value. It may be higher for existing companies, the difference being the share premium. The book value of ordinary shares refers to the paid-up capital plus reserves and surplus (net worth) divided by the number of outstanding shares. The price at which ordinary shares are traded in the stock market is their market value.

Ordinary shares have some special features in terms of the rights and claims of their holders: (a) residual claim to income/assets, (b) right to control, (c) pre-emptive rights, and (d) limited liability.

Ordinary shareholders have a residual claim to the income of the company. They are entitled to the remaining income/profits of the company after all outside claims are met. The amount actually received by the shareholders in the form of dividend depends on the decision of the board of directors. The directors have the right to decide what portion of the earning will be distributed to the shareholders as cash dividend and what portion will be ploughed back as retained earnings, which the shareholders may receive later in the form of capital appreciation/bonus shares.

The ordinary shareholders' claim in the assets of the company is also residual in that their claim would rank after the claims of the creditors and preference shareholders in the event of liquidation. If the liquidation value of assets is insufficient, their claims may remain unpaid.

As owners of the company, ordinary shareholders have the right to control the operations of, participate in the management of, the company. Their control is, however, indirect. The major policies/decisions are approved by the board of directors and the board-appointed management carries out the day-to-day operations. The shareholders have the legal right/power to elect the board of directors as well as vote on every resolution placed in various meetings of the company.

The ordinary shareholders exercise their right to control the company through voting in the meetings of the company.

According to the most commonly used system of voting in India, namely majority rule voting, each share carries one vote. As a result, shareholders/groups holding more than 50 percent of the outstanding equity shares are able to elect all the directors of their choice.

The ordinary shareholders of a company enjoy pre-emptive rights in the sense that they have a legal right to be offered, by the company, the first opportunity to purchase additional issues of equity capital in proportion to their existing holdings.

Although ordinary shareholders share the ownership risk, their liability is limited to the extent of their investment in the share capital of the company. See also Preference Shares.

Out-of-the-money (OTM) Option: An OTM is an option that would lead to a negative cash flow if it were exercised immediately. A call option on the index is out-of-the-money when the current index stands at a level that is less than the strike price (that is, spot price<strike price). If the index is much lower than the strike price, the call is said to be deep OTM. In the case of a put, the put is OTM if the index is above the strike price.

Over the Counter (OTC): A financial transaction that is not made on an organised exchange. Generally, the parties must negotiate all the details of each transaction or agree to use simplifying market conventions.

Pp

Paid-up Capital: The amount of capital, both equity and preference, paid-up by the shareholders against the capital subscribed to by them.

Par Value: Means the face value of securities.

Pari Passu: A term used to describe new issue of securities which have same rights as similar issues already in existence.

Participating Preference Shares: The right of certain preference shareholders to participate in profits after a specified fixed dividend contracted for is paid. Participation right is linked with the quantum of dividend paid on the equity shares over and above a particular specified level.

Partly Paid: Shares on which full nominal value has not been called up.

Pay in/Pay out: The days on which the members of a stock exchange pay or receive the amounts due to them are called pay in or pay out days respectively.

Payment Netting: Settling payments due on the same date and in the same currency on a net basis.

Pension Fund Regulatory and Development Authority (PFRDA): See Pension Funds, *168*.

Pension Funds: Pension sector reforms were initiated in India to establish a robust and sustainable social security arrangement in the country seeing that only about 12-13 percent of the total workforce was covered by any formal social security system. The New Pension System (NPS) was introduced by the Government from January 1, 2004 for new entrants to the Central Government service, except the Armed Forces, and was extended to the general public from May 1, 2009 on a voluntary basis. The features of the NPS design are self-sustainability, portability and scalability. Based on individual choice, it is envisaged as a low-cost and efficient pension system backed by sound regulation. As a pure "defined contribution" product with no defined benefit element, returns are totally market-related. The NPS provides various investment options and choices to individuals to switch over from one option to another or from one fund manager to another, subject to certain regulatory restrictions.

Pension Fund Regulatory and Development Authority (PFRDA): PFRDA set up as a regulatory body for the pension sector, is engaged in consolidating the initiatives taken so far regarding the full NPS architecture and expanding the reach of the NPS distribution network. The full NPS architecture comprising a Central Recordkeeping Agency (CRA), pension fund managers (PFMs), trustee bank, custodian and NPS Trust has been put in place and is fully operational. The National Securities Depository Limited (NSDL) has been selected as the CRA. The PFRDA has also appointed 6 pension fund managers (PFM) for the unorganized sector, namely UTI Retirement Solutions Ltd., SBI Pension Funds Pvt. Ltd., ICICI Prudential Life Insurance Company Ltd., IDFC Asset Management Company Ltd., Reliance Capital Asset Management Ltd. and Kotak Mahindra Asset Management Company Ltd., as pension fund sponsors under the NPS.

NPS implementation in the Central Government has stabilized with more than 5.64 lakh employees already covered. The NPS has also been well received by the State Governments and 23 State Governments/Union Territories have notified similar schemes for their new recruits under the ambit of the NPS. The PFRDA has been working with all the States to enable them to log on to the NPS architecture with ease. NPS Trust and CRA have been in continuous dialogue with State Governments/Union Territories for facilitating their entry into the NPS.

Efforts are under way to extend the reach of the NPS to new

segments like Central and State autonomous bodies and the organized sector and introduce micro-pension initiatives focusing on a low cost model of the NPS to be implemented through SHGs and similar bodies.

For all citizens including workers in the unorganized sector, the NPS is currently available through nearly 900 service provider (SP) branches of 21 points of presence (PoP). The PFRDA has also recently appointed the Department of Posts as PoP in addition to seven other financial institutions which will expand the PoP-SP network by more than five times. While Tier I, the non-withdrawable pension account under the NPS has been in operation since May 1, 2009, Tier II, the withdrawable account has been made operational from December 1, 2009. The PFRDA has also enhanced the maximum entry age into the NPS from 55 years to 60 years. These initiatives are expected to help realize the full potential of the NPS in terms of economies of scale and benefit the subscribers in terms of lower fees and charges and higher returns.

The pension fund managers manage three separate schemes consisting of three asset classes, namely: (i) equity, (ii) Government securities, and (iii) credit risk-bearing fixed income instruments, with the investment in equity subject to a cap of 50 percent. The fund managers will invest only in index funds that replicate either the BSE sensitive index or NSE Nifty 50 index. The subscriber will have the option to decide the investment mix of his pension wealth. In case the subscriber is unable/unwilling to exercise any choice regarding asset allocation, his contribution will be invested in accordance with the "auto choice" option with a predefined portfolio.

Pension reforms in India have made substantial progress. With the extension of the NPS to all citizens from May 1, 2009, every citizen in the country now has the opportunity to participate in a regulated pension market. This will contribute significantly to old age income security in the country.

Periodicity: It refers to the frequency with which the data are compiled. Periodicity specifications for flow data are given in terms of the longest interval to be represented by a single data point. Those for stock data are given in the form of the longest interval between compilations. For example, the specification of quarterly periodicity for balance of payments data means that one quarter is the longest interval that may be represented by a single estimate.

Perpetual Inventory Method: The process of deriving data on stocks from transaction data is known as the perpetual inventory method. Under this method, for which a stock estimate for some base point in time is required, the compiler may calculate the value of a stock at the end of a period as being equal to the value of the stock at the beginning of the period, plus the impact of transactions and non-transaction changes in the value of the stock during the period.

Person of Indian Origin (PIO): A citizen of any country other than Bangladesh or Pakistan, if: (i) he at any time held Indian passport, (ii) he or either of his parents or any of his grandparents was a citizen of India by virtue of the Constitution of India or the Citizenship Act, 1955, or (iii) the person is a spouse of an Indian citizen or a person referred to in sub-clause (i) or (ii).

Person Resident in India: It means: (i) a person residing in India for more than one hundred and eighty-two days during the course of the preceding financial year, (ii) any person or body corporate registered or incorporated in India, (iii) an office, branch or agency in India owned or controlled by a person resident outside India, (iv) an office, branch or agency outside India owned or controlled by a person resident in India.

Persons Acting in Concert (PAC): Individual(s)/company(ies)/ any other legal entity(ies) who are acting together for a common objective or for a purpose of substantial acquisition of shares or voting rights or gaining control over the target company pursuant to an agreement or understanding whether formal or informal.

Plain Vanilla Transactions: The most common and generally the simplest types of derivatives transaction. Plain vanilla is a relative concept, and no precise list of plain vanilla transactions exists. Transactions that have unusual or less common features are often called exotic or structured.

Players: A diverse range of intermediaries and institutional investors active in the capital market. This includes securities firms, broker dealers, commercial banks, merchant banks, unit trust/mutual fund etc.

Poison Pill: A defence technique in US when a company issues to its shareholders a special preferred dividend stock which is convertible, after a takeover, into the acquirer's shares. The successful bidder thus faces the prospect of heavy dilution.

Poop and Scoop: A highly illegal practice occurring mainly on the Internet. A small group of informed people attempt to push down a stock by spreading false information and rumours. If they are successful, they can purchase the stock at bargain prices.

Portfolio: A collection of securities owned by an individual or an institution (such as a mutual fund) that may include stocks, bonds and money market securities.

Portfolio Investment: Investment which goes into the financial sector in the form of treasury bonds and notes, stocks, money market placements, and bank deposits. Portfolio investment involves neither control of operations nor ownership of physical assets. It is generally contrasted with Foreign Direct Investment (FDI) (q.v.).

One of the major forces changing the face and structure of international capital markets since 1990s has been the flow of cross-border portfolio investments—especially by foreign institutional investors (FIIs), from developed countries to the developing countries. Portfolio investors provide institutional character to the capital markets, flavoured by highly intensive research and diversified investments. FII investments inject global liquidity into the markets, raise the price-earning ratio and thus reduce the cost of capital. From the perspective of FIIs, investments in various countries provide a measure of portfolio diversification and hedging as also to take advantage of arbitrage opportunities.

FIIs make investments in various countries to provide a measure of portfolio diversification and hedging to their assets. The forces driving the recent change in the investment portfolio of FIIs, as reflected in the growing emphasis on equities of emerging market economies, include *inter alia*: (a) increased accessibility of these markets after liberalisation, (b) improved marketability, (c) fewer problems relating to thin trading, and (d) improved macroeconomic fundamentals of these countries.

Portfolio Manager: Any person, who pursuant to a contract or agreement with a client, advises or directs or undertakes on behalf of the client the management or administration of a portfolio of securities or the funds of the client as the case may be.

Position Limit: The maximum number of listed option contracts on a single security which can be held by an investor or group of investors acting jointly.

Position Netting: The netting of payment instructions in respect of obligations between two or more parties, but which neither satisfies nor discharges those original obligations.

Position Trading: Type of trading involving the holding of open positions for an extended period of time.

Preference Shares: Preference shares (also called preferred stock) are a unique type of long-term capital market instruments in that they combine some of the features of ordinary shares as well as some features of debentures. Thus,

1. As a hybrid form of financial instrument, they are similar to debentures insofar as they carry a fixed rate of dividend.
2. They rank higher than ordinary shares as claimants to the income/assets of the company.
3. Generally, preference shareholders do not have voting rights.
4. They do not have a share in residual earnings/assets.
5. Dividend on preference shares is paid out of divisible/after tax profit.
6. Payment of preference dividend depends on the discretion of the management, i.e. it is not an obligatory payment and non-payment does not force insolvency/liquidation.
7. Irredeemable types of preference shares have no fixed maturity date.

Preference shares have a prior claim over ordinary shares both on the income and assets of the company. In other words, preference dividend must be paid in full before payment of any dividend on ordinary shares. In the event of liquidation, the whole of preference share capital must be paid before anything is paid to the ordinary shareholders. Thus, preference shares stand midway between debentures and ordinary shares as regards claims on the income and assets of the company. Stated in terms of risk perspective, preference shares are less risky than ordinary shares but more risky than debentures. See also Ordinary Shares

Preferential Allotment: Further issue of shares/securities—convertible into equity shares at a later date— to a select group of persons in preference to all the existing shareholders of the company.

Preferred Stock: See Preference Shares, *173*.

Premium: If an investor buys a security for a price above its eventual value at maturity he has paid a premium for it.

Price Band: The range within which the price of a security or the index of a currency is permitted to move within a given period.

Price Discovery: A general term for the process by which financial markets attain an equilibrium price, especially in the primary market. Usually refers to the incorporation of information into the price.

Price Earning Ratio: The ratio of the market price of the share to earnings per share. This measure is used by investment experts to compare the relative merits of a number of securities.

Price Priority: Price priority means that if two orders are entered into the system, the order having the best price gets the priority.

Price Rigging: When persons acting in concert with each other collude to artificially increase or decrease the prices of a security, the process is called price rigging.

Price Sensitive Information: Any information which relates directly or indirectly to a company and which, if published, is likely to materially affect the price of securities of the company.

Pricing Options: An option buyer has the right but not the obligation to exercise on the seller. The worst that can happen to a buyer is the loss of the premium paid by him. His downside is limited to this premium, but his upside is potentially unlimited. This optionally has a value expressed in terms of the option price. Just like in other free markets, it is the supply and demand in the secondary market that drives the price of an option. There are various models that help us get close to the true price of an option. Most of these are variants of the celebrated Black-Scholes Model for pricing European options.

Primary and Secondary Securities: Primary securities are created by real sector units of the economy (joint stock companies) engaged in the production of goods. Shares and debentures issued by companies are good examples of primary securities. Secondary securities are created by financial institutions or intermediaries who are not the ultimate borrowers of funds. These institutions raise funds from public to make investments in primary securities. Some examples of secondary securities are bank deposits, units of Unit Trust of India and shares of mutual funds.

Private Company and Public Limited Company: Private company means a company which: (a) restricts the right to transfer its shares, (b) limits the number of its members to fifty, and (c) prohibits any invitation to the public to subscribe for any shares in the company. The violation of these conditions will make it a public limited company.

Private Placement: There is a substantial scale of securities issuance taking place through the private placement route. The private placement route has become a mechanism where securities can be placed with a few wholesale buyers of securities, without incurring the overheads of the public issue.

Profit Taking: Realizing profits by closing out an existing position.

Programme Trading: A technique which uses decision rules, usually programmed on a computer, to generate trading decisions automatically.

Prospectus: Any document that includes any notice, circular, advertisement or other document inviting deposits from the public or inviting offers from the public for the subscription or purchase of any shares in, or debentures of, a body corporate.

Proxy: One who votes for and on behalf of a shareholder at the meeting of a company.

Proxy Battle: A battle between a company and some of its own shareholders. It starts with a group of dissident shareholders soliciting proxies in order to force through a shareholder resolution.

Public Announcement: It is an announcement made in the newspapers by the acquirer, primarily disclosing his intention to acquire shares of the target company from existing shareholders by means of an open offer.

Public Issue: An invitation by a company to public to subscribe to the securities offered through a prospectus.

Puffing Advertisement: Advertising or planting some news in the newspaper or in any media in respect of a proposed corporate action and later taking the stand that the board of directors did not approve the proposed corporate action. It can also mean news about financial results, given in misleading or distorted manner, intended to generate or induce trading in the scrip.

Pump and Dump: A highly illegal practice occurring mainly on the internet. A small group of informed people buy a stock before they recommend it to thousands of investors. The result is a quick spike in the price followed by an equally quick downfall. The people who have bought the stock early sell off when the price peaks.

Put Options: See Options, *158*.

Qq

Quasi Corporations: These are enterprises that produce goods and services in an economy other than their own, but do not establish separate legal corporations in the host country. Quasi corporations that are in a direct investment relationship with the parent enterprise are deemed to exist if: (a) production is maintained for one year or more, (b) a separate set of accounts is maintained for the local activities, and (c) income tax is paid in the host country. Quasi corporations are often involved in construction or the operation of mobile equipment in another economy.

Quotation: It may refer to specific market data relating to a security or commodity. While the term *quote* specifically refers to the bid price or ask price of an instrument, it may be more generically used to relate to the last price at which the security is traded at (last sale).

Rr

Radar Alter: It means close watch by the top management of a company on trading of its stock. The objective is to detect any unusual amount of buying which might indicate that some one is attempting to acquire a chunk of the stock in anticipation of a takeover attempt.

Random Walk Theory: It claims that a stock's past price action is no guide to future prices because prices move randomly, not in a pattern. Random walk theoreticians would sneer at the idea that because a stock has been moving up during the last few weeks it is likely to continue moving up.

Real Time Gross Settlement (RTGS) System: RTGS is a system for settlement of transactions for effective liquidity management by the members. The Indian RTGS system was operationalised in March 2004. The system started operations with four banks and settled only inter-bank transactions. Subsequently, the system was opened for settlement of customer transactions. It was operationalised for settlement of Multilateral Net Settlement Batch (MNSB) files from September 2006.

RTGS system is owned and operated by the Reserve Bank of India (RBI). The system works on a mainframe computer. Members are provided with a Participant Interface (PI), using which the participants connect to the system at the RBI through the INFINET. The message flow architecture in the RTGS system uses the Y topology. The members communicate through their PI to the Inter-bank Funds Transfer Processor (IFTP) which validates all communication and also does the *strip and store* function. Upon successful completion of a transaction and receipt of confirmation from the RTGS, the IFTP forwards the complete credit information to the beneficiary member's PI. All communication between the PI and IFTP and IFTP to RTGS uses digital signatures (Public Key Infrastructure) to ensure security.

The membership of RTGS is open to all scheduled commercial banks (SCBs), primary dealers (PDs) and others, as may be decided by the RBI. The SCBs are provided with Type A membership, primary dealers Type B and clearing houses Type D membership. Except Type A members, customer-based transactions cannot be submitted by other members. Type D members are permitted to submit only net settlement batches for settlement under the RTGS system. Other banks and financial institutions can participate as customers of the direct members.

RTGS operations are governed by the RTGS Membership Regulations, 2004 and RTGS (Membership) Business Operating Guidelines, 2004. The members of the system agree to abide by these regulations and guidelines and any subsequent amendments to these documents.

The settlement of RTGS transactions takes place in the books of the RBI. For this purpose, members have to open a 'RTGS Settlement Account' with the RBI at Mumbai. This account is to be funded at the beginning of each RTGS processing day from the member's current account with the RBI, and at the end of the day, the balance in the settlement account is transferred back to the current account of the member.

Members are provided with collateralized intra-day liquidity (IDL) facility to tide over their IDL mis-matches. This facility is provided to Type A and Type B members only. The IDL facility utilised by the members has to be necessarily reversed by them at the end of RTGS day. Failure to do so attracts penal action.

In addition to IDL, the system provides many features for effective liquidity management by the members. These include message release method, queuing management and queue visibility. The Indian RTGS has adopted the FIFO rule for queuing. The system has a centralised queuing arrangement with priorities assigned by the system participant. The participant/system operator can change the priority of messages/revoke the messages in the queue. The system operator would alter the queue only in extreme situations. At the end of the day, all pending unsettled messages are cancelled by the system.

The system has a multilateral offsetting algorithm to resolve any gridlock situations that may arise. This process can be configured to be invoked manually or automatically by the system. Since it is mainly a large-value funds transfer system, a floor of ₹ 1 lakh has been prescribed for minimum value of transactions that can be settled through RTGS.

There has been a substantial increase in the volume of transactions settled through RTGS. The inter-bank clearing at all the RBI centres have been migrated to the RTGS system. Further, multilateral net settlements from Clearing Corporation of India Limited (CCIL)—viz. rupee leg of US dollar-Indian rupee settlement, funds leg of government securities settlement and funds leg of Collateralised Borrowing and Lending Obligations (CBLO)—and the retail net settlement systems operated by National Clearing Cell, Mumbai (MICR cheque clearing, high value clearing, National Electronic Funds Transfer (NEFT) and Electronic Clearing Services (ECS) are settled in RTGS as multilateral net settlement batch (MNSB) files. The liquidity management operations of the RBI are also settled through the RTGS system.

Record Date: A date on which the records of a company are closed for the purpose of determining the stockholders to whom dividends, proxies, rights etc., are to be sent.

Redemption Price: It is the price at which a bond is redeemed.

Regional Financial Integration: It occurs due to ties between a given region and the major financial centre serving that region. Economic integration might be easier to achieve at a regional level due to network externalities and the tendency of market makers to concentrate in certain geographical centres. Furthermore, regional financial integration can be an important means of developing local financial markets, for instance, through peer pressure to strengthen institutions and upgrade local practices.

Registered Bonds: A bond which is registered in the books of the company in the name of the owner.

Registrar to an Issue: The person appointed by a body corporate or any person or group of persons to: (a) carry on the activities of collecting applications from investors in respect of an issue, (b) keeping a proper record of applications and monies received from investors, (c) assisting body corporate or person or group of persons in determining the basis of allotment of securities in consultation with the stock exchange, (d) finalising of the list of persons entitled to allotment of securities, and (e) processing and despatching allotment letters, refund orders or certificates and other related documents in respect of the issue.

Rematerialisation: Rematerialisation is the term used for converting electronic holdings back into certificates. If the investor wishes to get back his securities in physical form, all he has to do is to request his depository participant (DP) for rematerialisation of the same. An investor's DP will forward his request to National Securities Depository Limited (NSDL). After verifying that he has the necessary balance, NSDL in turn will intimate the registrar who will print the certificates and dispatch the same to the investor.

Repo: See Repurchase Agreement, *182*.

Repurchase Agreement (Repo): It is a money market instrument, which enables collaboralised short-term borrowing and lending through sale/purchase operations in debt instruments. Under a repo transaction, a holder of securities sells them to an investor with an agreement to repurchase at a pre-determined date and rate. In the case of a repo, the forward clean price of the bonds is set in advance at a level which is different from the spot clean price by adjusting the difference between repo interest and coupon earned on the security. Repo is also called a ready forward transaction as it is a means of funding by selling a security held on a spot (ready) basis and repurchasing the same on a forward basis.

Reverse repo is a mirror image of repo as in the case of former, securities are acquired with a simultaneous commitment to resell.

In India, banks often entered into buy back arrangements in respect of Government and other approved securities and PSU bonds among themselves and with their large public sector and corporate clients until April 15, 1987 when the RBI issued certain guidelines prohibiting buy back arrangements in respect of corporate securities and bonds issued by public sector undertakings. From December 1, 1987 the units of Unit Trust of India were not eligible as approved security for the purpose of entering into repo transactions. In order to ward off any undesirable developments following the detection of large scale misuse of repos, banks were prohibited from entering into buy back arrangements in Government and other approved securities with non-bank clients, while they could enter into buyback arrangements with other banks (inter-bank) with effect from April 4, 1988.

Repo/reverse repo operations are also undertaken by the RBI as part of its open market operations. The RBI initially conducted repo operations for a period of 14 days. Since November 1996, the RBI has been conducting 3-4 day repo auctions, synchronizing with working day and week-end liquidity conditions, in order to modulate short-term liquidity. With the introduction of liquidity adjustment facility (LAF) from June 5, 2000, the RBI has been injecting liquidity into the system through repos on a daily basis. These operations are conducted on all working days except on Saturdays, through uniform price auctions and are restricted to scheduled commercial banks and PDs.

To develop and widen the repos market, the RBI introduced regulatory safeguards such as delivery versus payments (DvP) system in April 1999. The operationalisation of Negotiated Dealing System (NDS) and the Clearing Corporation of India Ltd. (CCIL) provided a further boost to this market.

Being a money market instrument, regulation of the repo market falls under the RBI's jurisdiction. Accordingly, the RBI is concerned with use of repo as an instrument by banks or non-bank entities and issues relating to type of eligible instruments for undertaking repo and eligibility of participants to undertake such transactions. It has been issuing instructions in this regard to banks, in consultation with the Central Government.

Repurchase Price: The price or net asset value at which an open-ended scheme purchases or redeems its units from the unit holders. It may include exit load, if applicable.

Reserve Bank of India (RBI): The Reserve Bank of India Act was placed on the statute book on March 6, 1934. The RBI commenced operations on April 1, 1935 and was nationalised on January 1, 1949. The head office of the Bank is in Mumbai and its executive head is called the Governor.

The objective of establishing the RBI, as stated in the preamble to the RBI Act 1934, was to "regulate the issue of bank notes and the keeping of the reserves with a view to securing monetary stability in India and generally to operate the currency and credit system of the country to its advantage". The Bank's functions as laid down in the statutes were: (a) issue of currency, (b) banker to Government, and (c) banker to other banks. Except in the sphere of agriculture, the Bank was not entrusted with any great promotional role and that too on a limited scale.

Functions of RBI: The RBI performs all the major functions of a central bank and these are discussed below.

***Sole Currency Authority*:** Barring one-rupee notes and coins, RBI is the sole authority for the issue of currency in India. One rupee notes and coins are issued by the Central Government. However, their distribution to the public is the sole responsibility of the RBI. For the issue of notes, the RBI has a separate department, the Department of Issue. All the currency issued by the RBI is its monetary liability and is backed by assets of equal value.

Banker to the Governments: Before the formation of the RBI, the Imperial Bank of India performed many of the functions as banker to the Government. With the establishment of the RBI, the Imperial Bank ceased to be the banker to the Government, but entered into an agreement with the RBI for providing its services as the sole agent of the RBI in places where it had a branch and there was no branch of the Banking Department of the RBI.

As the banker to the Central Government and to the State Governments by virtue of agreements entered into with them, the RBI provides a range of banking services for these Governments such as acceptance of money on government account payment/withdrawals of funds and collection and transfer of funds through different means. Sections 20, 21 and 21A of the RBI Act provide the statutory basis for these functions. The terms and conditions on which the RBI acts as banker to the Central and State Governments are set out in separate agreements, which the RBI entered into with these Governments.

Presently, RBI is the banker for all Governments in India (except Jammu and Kashmir). The RBI provides all those banking services to the Central and State Governments which a commercial bank ordinarily offers to its customers. The Governments keep their cash balances on current account deposit with the RBI and the latter carries out banking business involving receipts and payments of money on behalf of the Governments. The Governments are required, under agreement, to maintain a minimum balance with the RBI. It is the duty of the Finance Department of each Government to ensure that there are always sufficient funds in its bank account and that at no stage the cash balance falls short of the prescribed minimum.

Bankers' Bank and Lender-of-the-last-resort: Under the Reserve Bank of India Act, 1934 and the Banking Regulation Act, 1949, the RBI is vested with extensive powers of supervision, regulation, and control over commercial and co-operative banks. The regulatory functions of the RBI pertain to licensing, branch expansion, and amalgamation of commercial banks. The RBI calls for returns and other information from the commercial banks and periodically inspects their working.

The scheduled banks in India are required under law to deposit with the RBI a stipulated ratio (lying between 3 percent and 15 percent) of their total liabilities. These are compulsory reserves of banks with the RBI and are not available to them for meeting inter-bank clearing claims. The underlying philosophy of this statutory reserve requirement is that by varying it within limits, the RBI can use it as a weapon of monetary-credit control.

Reserves of the banks with the RBI may be used to meet the temporary cash needs of the commercial banks. Commercial banks are supposed to meet their shortfalls of cash from sources other than the RBI but in acute emergency they can approach the RBI for help and that is why the central bank is also called the lender-of-the-last-resort.

Controller of Money and Credit: An important function of RBI is to control money and credit in the country. The instruments of monetary control operated by the RBI may be classified into two categories: (a) quantitative or global or aggregative measures which affect the total amount of money supply and credit, and (b) qualitative or selective measures which affect the allocation of bank credit among competing uses and users.

A. Quantitative Credit Controls: These are the following.

1. **Bank Rate:** As the lender-of-the-last-resort, the RBI helps the commercial banks in temporary need of cash when other sources of raising cash are exhausted. The RBI provides credit to banks by rediscounting eligible bills of exchange and by making advances against eligible securities such as government securities. The lending rate for these advances by the RBI is called the bank rate which is a traditional weapon to control money supply. An increase in the bank rate would discourage commercial banks to borrow from the RBI and a corresponding increase in the lending rate of commercial banks to general public would decrease public borrowings from the banks.
2. **Cash Reserve Ratio (CRR)**: Scheduled banks in India are required statutorily to hold cash reserves, called cash reserve ratio (CRR), with the RBI. Increase/decrease in CRR is used by the RBI as an instrument of monetary control, particularly to mop up excess increases in the supply of money. This

power was given to RBI in 1956.

3. **Statutory Liquidity Ratio (SLR):** Apart from the CRR, banks in India are also subject to statutory liquidity requirement. Under this requirement, commercial banks along with other financial institutions like Life Insurance Corporation of India, the General Insurance Corporation and the provident funds are required under law to invest prescribed minimum proportions of their total assets/liabilities in government securities and other approved securities. The underlying philosophy of this provision is to allocate total bank credit between the government and the rest of the economy. The assurance of a certain minimum share of bank credit to the government affects the borrowings of the government from the RBI and hence serves as a tool of quantitative monetary control. The SLR provision has created a captive market for government securities which increases automatically with the growth in the liabilities of the banks. Moreover, it has kept the cost of the debt to the government low in view of the generally low rate of interest on government securities.
4. **Open Market Operations:** The RBI can enter the money market for the purpose of purchase or sale of Government securities on its own account. Every open market purchase by the RBI increases primary money by equal amount while every sale decreases it. As regards their advantages, open market operations are highly flexible, easily reversible in time, their effect on money supply is immediate, and they do not carry *announcement effects* as in the case of changes in the bank rate. Open market operations, considered very effective in developed countries, are not of much importance in India in view of the captive nature of the market for Government bonds. For example, the treasury bill market is limited largely to the RBI itself and scheduled commercial banks which are required under law to invest a certain minimum proportion of their total liabilities in Government securities. The private dealers in Government securities are

few and far between.

5. **Moral Suasions:** Through moral suasions (discussions, suggestions and advice), the RBI can influence the investment and credit policies of the commercial banks. For example, it can ask the commercial banks to invest a larger proportion, than required, of their assets in Government securities. Similarly, it can advise them regarding the allocation of credit to the private sector.

B. Selective Credit Controls (SCCs): SCCs, introduced in India in 1956, pertain to regulation of credit for specific purposes. The techniques of SCCs used by the RBI include fixing minimum margins for lending against securities, ceiling on maximum advances to individual borrowers against stocks of certain commodities, and minimum discriminatory rates of interest prescribed for certain kinds of advances. SCCs have been used mainly to prevent the speculative holding of essential commodities like foodgrains to prevent price rise.

Selective credit controls were abolished in the wake of economic reforms programme initiated in early 1990s.

Controller of Foreign Exchange: The RBI is the custodian of the foreign exchange reserves of India. It manages exchange control and the external value of the rupee. The history of exchange control in India dates back to the outbreak of Second World War in 1939. The exchange control is operated in a manner so that the demand for foreign exchange is contained within the limits of its available supplies. In other words, the available foreign exchange is allocated among competing demands in such a way as to make its optimum use. The need for this control and planned use arises in view of the general shortage of foreign exchange reserves in most developing countries. All foreign exchange transactions made by the RBI are at the official rates of exchange.

The RBI has delegated considerable powers to the authorised dealers to release foreign exchange for a variety of purposes and has been focusing on the development of the foreign exchange market. In order to deepen the foreign exchange market, a large number of products have been introduced and the entry of newer players has been allowed. Additional hedging instruments, such as, foreign currency-rupee options have been introduced and authorised dealers have been permitted to use innovative products like cross-currency options, interest rate and currency swaps, caps/collars and forward rate agreements (FRAs) in the international forex market.

Source of Economic Information: The RBI provides, through its publications, useful data and information on various aspects of the economy, particularly monetary and banking activities. Three important and regular publications of the RBI are: (a) Reserve Bank of India *Bulletin* (Monthly), (b) *Report on Currency and Finance* (Annual), and (c) *Handbook of Statistics on Indian Economy.*

Promotional Role of RBI: Apart from performing the customary functions of a central bank, the RBI has played an important role in building, consolidating, and strengthening the financial infrastructure of India. It has also played an effective role in influencing the allocation of credit in favour of priority sectors. Commercial banking facilities have been extended to small towns and rural areas as a result of the policies of the RBI.

The RBI has paid special attention to the credit needs of the rural (agricultural) sector. Towards this end, the Agricultural Refinance and Development Corporation (ARDC) was set up as a wholly-owned subsidiary of the RBI in 1963. The National Bank for Agriculture and Rural Development (NABARD) is another example of the promotional role of the RBI in the agricultural sector. Similarly, the RBI promoted the cause of industrial finance by actively associating itself with such public sector undertakings as erstwhile Industrial Development Bank of India (IDBI). In the area of credit allocation, RBI has followed the policy of special consideration for priority sectors at concessional rates of interest.

Restructuring: A restructured account is one where the bank, grants to the borrower concessions that the bank would not otherwise consider. Restructuring would normally involve modification of terms of the advances/securities, which would generally include, among others, alteration of repayment period/repayable amount/the amount of instalments and rate of interest. It is a mechanism to nurture an otherwise viable unit, which has been adversely impacted, back to health.

Resurgent India Bonds (RIBs), 1998: The issue of RIBs was contemplated in view of extraordinary developments in 1998-99, when a shortfall in capital flows consequent upon imposition of sanctions, especially debt flows, in relation to current account deficit was anticipated. Instead of drawing down foreign exchange reserves which could have adversely affected market sentiments, or reducing the current account deficit through drastic import cuts which would have affected real economic activity, it was felt that RIBs would enhance the debt flows at the least possible cost. It was envisaged that such borrowings could offset the adverse market sentiment created in international capital markets in the light of the downgrading of India's sovereign rating to non-investment grade. This could have been done by demonstrably raising debt resources at a cost lower than that any organised financial intermediary was prepared to provide in the context of the rating downgrade. At the same time, it was necessary to ensure that amounts so obtained were restricted quantitatively to meet essential needs as a replacement for normal debt flows, by keeping an option for premature closure.

Furthermore, by keeping the maturity of RIBs to five years, it was ensured that the borrowing had an appropriate medium-term maturity. The success of RIBs could be gauged from the substantial amount of funds mobilised (US$ 4.2 billion) in the international market at a competitive rate. The RIBs were redeemed on October 1, 2003 without any pressure on the exchange rate and liquidity conditions.

Retained Earnings: The term refers to profit after tax minus dividend paid/proposed.

Revaluation Reserves: Revaluation reserves are a part of Tier II capital. These reserves arise from revaluation of assets that are undervalued on the bank's books, typically bank premises and marketable securities. The extent to which the revaluation reserves can be relied upon as a cushion for unexpected losses depends mainly upon the level of certainty that can be placed on estimates of the market values of the relevant assets and the subsequent deterioration in values under difficult market conditions or in a forced sale.

Reverse Book Building: Reverse book building is similar to the process of book building, which is aimed at securing the optimum price for a company's share. In reverse book building the investors' aim is to sell the shares to exit the company.

Reverse Repo: See Repurchase Agreement (Repo), *182*.

Rigged Market: Manipulation of share price to attract buyers and sellers to the riggers advantage.

Rights Issue: The issue of new securities to existing shareholders in a fixed ratio to those already held.

Risk Management: The principal benefit of the derivatives market is that it provides the opportunity for risk management through hedging. Derivatives are innovations in risk management not in risk itself. Risk management in any type of institution is a continuous process and not a one-time activity. It has three distinctive sequential steps: (a) risk identification, (b) risk measurement, and (c) risk mitigation.

Risk can be defined as the possibility and probability of loss. These are: (a) credit risk, (b) market risk, and (c) operational risk.

Derivatives can be used to hedge both credit and market risks. While credit risk represents the conventional counter party risk, market risk refers to all those market forces/variables which may adversely affect an institution's profitability and economic value.

Market risk is characteristically represented by price risk of all types, viz. interest rate risk, exchange rate risk, commodity price risk, equity price risk etc. While credit and market risks are external, operational risks are those risks which are essentially internal to an organization. Derivatives are of little help in hedging such types of risks.

Rolling Settlement: The practice on many stock markets of settling a transaction a fixed number of days after the trade is agreed.

Ruling Price: It means the current market price of a security.

Run: A run involves a person creating activity in a security by successively buying or selling that security. The intention is that the increased activity would, in case where the person is buying, attract others to buy and push up the price. At that point, those organizing the run would then attempt to sell out at a financial gain. This is sometimes known as *pumping and dumping*.

Ss

Safe Harbour: Another way of fighting off an unfriendly takeover by a company. Here, the company that is the object of the takeover goes out and buys a radio station, airline, or similar business, under the assumption that ownership of a subsidiary in such a heavily regulated industry will make acquisition of the company less attractive.

Satellite Banking: Having regard to much greater reliability of a satellite-based communication link for interconnecting the branches of the banks, particularly in the hilly areas and difficult terrain where terrestrial communication link is difficult to provide, the RBI had constituted a Technical Group to examine the proposal for providing satellite connectivity to the bank branches in such areas. The objective is to enable greater penetration of the electronic payment products in the hinterland areas also, by facilitating the integration of the rural and remote branches with the core banking solution platform of the banks and help them providing efficient banking services to their customers. Under the proposal, the RBI would be bearing a part of the leased rentals for the satellite connectivity, provided the banks use it for connecting their branches in the North Eastern States and in the under-banked districts in the rest of the country. Thus, the RBI would be providing an incentive to the banks for adopting the satellite communication technology for networking their branches in the remote areas. A discussion paper on this scheme was placed on RBI website in June 2008 for public comments.

Sauda Book: Members and authorized assistants are given a book called *Sauda Book* to record transactions of sales and purchases.

Scenario Analysis: A method in which the earnings or value impact is computed for different interest rate scenario.

Screen-based Trading: Form of trading that uses modern telecommunication and computer technology to combine information transmission with trading in financial markets.

SEBI: See Securities and Exchange Board of India, *194*.

Secondary Market: The market for previously issued securities or financial instruments.

Sector Fund: A fund that invests primarily in securities of companies engaged in a specific investment segment. Sector funds entail more risk, but may offer greater potential returns than funds that diversify their portfolios.

Securities: Under Section 2 of the Securities Contracts (Regulation) Act, 1956, securities include the following:

1. Shares, scrips, stocks, bonds, debentures, debenture stocks, or other marketable securities of a like nature in or of any incorporated company or other body corporate.
2. Government securities.
3. Such other instruments as may be declared by the Central Government to be securities.
4. Rights or interests in securities.

Government Security: It means a security created and issued, whether before or after the commencement of the Securities Contracts (Regulations) Act, 1956 by the Central Government or a State Government for the purpose of raising a public loan and having one of the forms specified in Section 2(2) of the Public Debt Act, 1944. See also Government Securities.

Securities and Exchange Board of India (SEBI): In 1992, the Capital Issues (Control) Act, 1947 was repealed and the office of the Controller of Capital Issues (CCIs) was abolished.

The Securities and Exchange Board of India (SEBI) was constituted on April 12, 1988 as a non-statutory body through an Administrative Resolution of the Government for dealing with all matters relating to development and regulation of the securities market and investor protection and to advise the government on all these matters. SEBI was given statutory status and powers through an Ordinance promulgated on January 30, 1992. SEBI was established as a statutory body on February 21, 1992. The Ordinance was replaced by Securities and Exchange Board of India Act 1992 on April 4, 1992.

With this ended all controls related to raising of funds from the market. The move was aimed at enhancing the efficiency, safety, integrity and transparency of the market. Presently, issuers of capital are required to meet the guidelines of SEBI on disclosures and protection of investors.

SEBI has emerged as an autonomous and independent statutory body. Its legally mandated objectives are the following:

1. Protection of the interests of investors in securities.
2. Development of the securities market.
3. Regulation of the securities market.
4. Matters connected therewith and incidental thereto.

The SEBI prohibits fraudulent and unfair trade practices, including insider trading. It also regulates substantial acquisition of shares and takeovers. In order to ensure protection of investors and to safeguard the integrity of the markets, there is a comprehensive surveillance system. Stock exchanges are the primary targets for detection of market manipulation, price rigging and other regulatory breaches regarding capital market functioning.

The SEBI regulates and supervises the securities market through its various regulations, guidelines and schemes issued from time to time.

The powers and functions of SEBI—as the securities market regulator—have been laid down in the SEBI Act, 1992. SEBI also exercises powers under the Securities Contracts (Regulation) Act, 1956, the Depositories Act, 1996 and certain provisions of the Companies Act, 1956. It regulates the securities markets, securities market institutions and market intermediaries, such as the stock exchanges, depositories, mutual funds and other asset management companies, securities dealers and brokers, merchant bankers, credit rating agencies and venture capital funds.

The statutory powers and functions of SEBI were strengthened through the promulgation of the Securities Laws (Amendment) Ordinance on January 25, 1995, which was subsequently replaced by an Act of Parliament.

The SEBI is equipped with the following powers:

1. Powers to register and regulate, inspect, enquire and investigate and undertake audits, and to cancel registration (though in this last case this applies to the mutual fund rather than the AMC); also to prohibit issue of an offer document including prospectus or advertisement.
2. Powers to summon and enforce attendance and examine on oath, inspect registers and documents, discover and enforce disclosure of books of account and other documents.
3. Powers to restrain from business, suspend, search, impound and retain proceeds, access bank data and attach bank accounts, prevent alienation of assets and issue cease and desist orders.
4. Powers to require compensation to be paid to investors.

Those who appeal against SEBI judgements are heard by the Securities Appellate Tribunal (SAT) and can also go to the Supreme Court if they do not accept the Tribunal's judgement.

The SAT has three members, one of whom is required to be the presiding officer who is a sitting or retired judge of the Supreme Court or High Court.

The two other members must be of ability, integrity and standing with experience of corporate law, securities law, finance, economics or accountancy.

SEBI has regional offices in five cities—Mumbai, New Delhi, Chennai, Kolkata and Ahmedabad.

The experience of SEBI during episodes of market misconduct revealed many limitations in the legal provisions of the SEBI Act. In addition, the growing importance of the securities markets in the economy has placed new demands upon SEBI. On October 28, 2002, an ordinance was promulgated which sought to strengthen SEBI. This ordinance involved organisational strengthening of SEBI, giving SEBI more powers for investigations and penalties, and making clearer concepts like insider trading and market manipulations.

The regulatory ambit has been widened in tune with the emerging needs and developments in the equity markets. Apart from stock exchanges, various intermediaries such as mutual funds, stock brokers and sub-brokers, merchant bankers, portfolio managers, registrars to an issue, share transfer agents, underwriters, debentures trustees, bankers to an issue, custodian of securities, venture capital funds and issuers have been brought under the SEBI's regulatory purview.

Securities and Exchange Commission (SEC): It is the US Government agency that regulates securities trading. It has civil enforcement powers only and must seek criminal prosecution through the US Justice Department.

Securities Lending Scheme: A scheme formed in 1997 for lending of securities through an approved intermediary to a borrower under an agreement for a specified period with the condition that the borrower will return equivalent securities of the same type or class at the end of the specified period along with the corporate benefits accruing on the securities borrowed.

Securitisation: See Asset Securitisation, *8*.

Securitisation, Reconstruction of Financial Assets and Enforcement of Security Interest (SARFAESI) Act, 2002: The enactment of SARFAESI Act, 2002 was an important landmark in the ongoing reforms in the financial sector. The Act enables the setting up of asset management companies, addressing the problem of non-performing assets (NPAs) of banks and financial institutions and enhancing creditor rights. The main provisions of the Act are as follows.

1. A securitisation company or reconstruction company having

own funds of not less than ₹ 2 crore or such other amount not exceeding 15 percent of total financial assets acquired or to be acquired as specified by the RBI can commence business after obtaining a certificate of registration, subject to fulfilling certain conditions and complying with the prudential norms set by the RBI.

2. The securitisation or reconstruction company may acquire assets of any bank or financial institution by issuing a debenture or bond or any other security for consideration agreed upon between such company and the bank or the financial institution.
3. Notice of acquisition of a financial asset may be sent by bank or financial institution to an obligor. The obligor on receipt of such notice will make payment to the securitisation company concerned.
4. A securitisation company may raise funds from qualified institutional buyers by formulating schemes for acquiring financial assets.
5. In the event of non-realisation of financial assets, qualified institutional buyers of a securitisation company holding not less than 75 percent of the total value of securities issued by such company are entitled to call for a meeting of all institutional buyers and the resolution passed in such a meeting is binding on the company.
6. A securitisation or a reconstruction company may provide for the proper management of the business of the borrower, sale or lease of a part or whole of the business of borrower, settlement of dues payable by the borrower and taking possession of secured assets within the framework of guidelines framed by the RBI.
7. Other functions of the securitisation company include acting as an agent for any bank or financial institution for the purpose of recovery of their dues.
8. Secured creditor is entitled to enforce any security interest created in its favour without the intervention of the court or tribunal.

9. In case of non-performing debts, the secured creditor is entitled to serve a notice to the borrower to discharge his liabilities within 60 days.
10. In case of failure to discharge the liabilities in the stipulated period, the secured creditor is entitled to take possession of secured assets, take over the management of secured assets and to appoint any person to manage the same.
11. Borrowers are entitled to prefer an appeal with the Debts Recovery Tribunal after depositing 75 percent of the amount claimed by the secured creditor. Borrowers aggrieved by the order of the Debts Recovery Tribunal may prefer an appeal to an Appellate Tribunal within 30 days from the date of receipt of the order of Debts Recovery Tribunal.

Settlement Advisory Committees have also been formed at regional and head office levels of commercial banks. Furthermore, banks can also issue notices under the Securitisation and Reconstruction of Financial Assets and Enforcement of Security Interest (SARFAESI) Act, 2002 for enforcement of security interest without intervention of courts. Thus, banks have a menu of options to resolve their problem of NPAs.

With a view to providing an additional option and developing a healthy secondary market for NPAs, guidelines on sale/purchase of non-performing assets were issued in July 2005 where securitisation companies and reconstruction companies are not involved. The draft guidelines cover the following broad areas: (a) procedure for purchase/sale of non-performing financial assets by banks, including valuation and pricing aspects, and (b) prudential norms relating to asset classification, provisioning, accounting of recoveries, capital adequacy and exposure norms and disclosure requirements.

The guidelines include several specific provisions, including the following.

1. A non-performing asset in the books of a bank shall be eligible for sale to other banks only if it has remained a non-performing asset for at least two years in the books of the selling bank and such selling should be only on a cash basis.

2. A non-performing financial asset should be held by the purchasing bank in its books at least for a period of 15 months before it is sold to other banks.
3. A bank may purchase/sell non-performing financial assets from/to other banks only on a 'without recourse' basis.
4. Banks should ensure that subsequent to sale of the non-performing financial assets to other banks, they do not have any involvement with reference to assets sold and do not assume operational, legal or any other type of risks relating to the financial assets sold.
5. A non-performing financial asset may be classified as 'standard' in the books of the purchasing bank for a period of 90 days from the date of purchase. Thereafter, the asset classification status of the account shall be determined by the record of recovery in the books of the purchasing bank with reference to cash flows estimated while purchasing the asset. The asset shall attract provisioning requirement appropriate to its asset classification status in the books of the purchasing bank.
6. Any recovery in respect of a non-performing asset purchased from other banks should first be adjusted against its acquisition cost. Recoveries in excess of the acquisition cost can be recognised as profit.
7. The asset classification status of an existing exposure to the same obligor in the books of the purchasing bank will continue to be governed by the record of recovery of that exposure and hence may be different.
8. For the purpose of capital adequacy, banks should assign 100 percent risk weights to the non-performing financial assets purchased from other banks.
9. In the case the non-performing asset purchased is an investment, then it would attract capital charge for market risks also.
10. Purchasing bank should ensure compliance with the prudential credit exposure ceilings (both single and group) after reckoning the exposures to the obligors arising on

account of the purchase.

The RBI and the Central Government have initiated several institutional measures to contain the levels of NPAs, including the following.

1. Corporate Debt Restructuring (CDR) (q.v.).
2. Debt Recovery Tribunals (DRTs) (q.v.).
3. *Lok Adalats* (people's court) (q.v.).

Security Audit Trail: A security audit refers to an independent review and examination of records and activities of a system, in order to test for adequacy of system controls. It ensures compliance with established policy and operational procedures, to detect breaches in security, and to recommend any indicated changes in the control, policy and procedures. Audit trail refers to data generated by the system, which facilitates a security audit at a future date.

Self-clearing Member: A member of a clearing corporation or clearing house of the derivatives exchange or derivatives segment of a stock exchange who may clear and settle transactions on its own account or on account of its clients only, and shall not clear or settle transactions in securities for any other trading members.

Self-help Group (SHG): A self-help group (SHG) is a small voluntary association of 10-20 poor people from the same socio-economic background who come together for the purpose of addressing their common socio-economic problems through self-help and mutual-help. They collect small savings (thrift) on regular basis. Out of the pooled money, small interest bearing loans are given to the members and some amount is deposited with a bank regularly. The bank lends money for economic activities of the group without collateral security and at market rates. The savings of poor members are pooled resources saved with great difficulty. This hard-earned money is termed as *warm money*. The money obtained by the group from outsiders, i.e. banks, micro finance institutions is termed as *cold money*.

Members make small regular contributions over a few months until there is enough capital with the group to begin lending. Funds may then be lent back to the members or to others in the village for any purpose. In India, many SHGs are *linked* to banks for the delivery of micro credit.

SHGs are started by non-governmental organizations (NGOs) that generally have broad anti-poverty agendas. SHGs are seen as instruments for a variety of goals including empowering women, developing leadership abilities among poor people, increasing school enrolments, and improving nutrition and the use of birth control. Financial intermediation is generally seen more as an entry point to these other goals, rather than as a primary objective.

SHGs have been instrumental in initiating micro entrepreneurial activities among those poor people who have been neglected so far and far away from the process of social as well economic development. Self-help Group-Bank Linkage Programme is responsible for developing banking habits among the poorest of the poor people.

The basic objective of self-help group is upliftment of poor people by means of micro economic activities so that the members get job opportunities, sustainable income and some assets for generation of regular income. There is tremendous enthusiasm in formation of the groups but care is not taken for their proper growth and survival.

The most significant contribution of SHGs is that they have been instrumental in building up enough confidence among the poor people and now they are ready to participate in the process of development. Many of these have been running fair price shops very successfully. A sizable number of the groups are working as caterers for the State Government-sponsored Mid-Day Meal Scheme. It is noteworthy that a good number of the SHGs have been marketing successfully the products of domestic as well as multinational corporations in remote rural areas.

Selling Short: A manner in which an investor sells securities he does not posses in the hope of buying them back later at a lower price.

Sensex: See Bombay Stock Exchange (BSE), *25*.

Series: All option contracts of the same classes that have the same expiration date and strike price.

Settlement Cycle: Following the enactment of the Depository Act, 1996, two depositories were set up: Central Depository Services Ltd. (CDSL) and National Securities Depository Ltd. (NSDL). The CDSL and NSDL have been successful in the dematerialisation of securities almost to the full extent. Presently, the transfer of ownership is mostly done through book-entry form. This has greatly improved the speed, accuracy and security of the settlement system. Prior to these arrangements, the settlement cycle was as high as 14 days for specified scrips and 30 days for others. The settlement risk was very high because of unforeseen happenings between the transaction and the settlement. To begin with, the settlement cycle was reduced to a week. Thereafter, rolling settlement was introduced on a T+5 basis in July 2001. From December 2001, all scrips which had established connectivity with the above-mentioned Depositories were moved to rolling settlement. The settlement cycle was further reduced to T+3 in April 2002 and to T+2 in April 2003.

Settlement Date: The date specified for delivery of securities between securities firms.

Settlement Period: For administrative convenience, a stock exchange divides the year into a number of settlement periods so as to enable members to settle their trades. All transactions executed during the settlement period are settled at the end of the settlement period.

Settlement Risk (Principal Risk): The risk that the seller of a security delivers its obligation but does not receive payment or that the buyer of a security makes payment but does not receive delivery. In this event, the full principal value of the securities transferred is at risk.

Share Transfer Agent: Any person who, on behalf of any body corporate, maintains the record of holders of securities issued by such body corporate and deals with all matters connected with the transfer and redemption of its securities. It can also be a department or division of a body corporate performing the above activities.

Short Covering: Buying of stocks by a seller to complete his previous commitments.

Short Position: In futures, the short has sold the commodity or security for future delivery; in options, the short has sold the call or the put and is obligated to take a futures position if he or she is assigned for exercise.

Short Squeeze: A situation in which a lack of supply and an excess demand for a traded stock forces the price upward. If a stock price starts to rise rapidly, the trend may continue to escalate because the short sellers will likely want out. For example, say a stock rises 15 percent in one day, those with short positions may be forced to liquidate and cover their position by purchasing the stock. If enough short sellers buy back the stock, the price is pushed even higher.

Special Economic Zone (SEZ): It is a geographical region governed by the SEZ Act, 2005 that is deemed to be foreign territory for the purposes of trade operations, duties and tariffs to enhance foreign investment and promote exports from the country.

Special Purpose Vehicle (SPV): An entity which may be a trust, company or other entity constituted or established by a *deed* or *agreement* for a specific purpose.

Specified Shares: A group of equity shares in which carry forward of transactions from one settlement period to the next is permitted.

Speculators: If hedgers are the people who wish to avoid the price risk, speculators are those who are willing to take such risk. These are the people who take position in the market and assume risks to profit from fluctuations in prices. In fact, the speculators consume information, make forecasts about the prices and put their money in these forecasts. Depending on their perceptions, they may take long or short positions on futures and/or options, or may hold spread positions (simultaneous long and short positions on the same derivatives).

Speculators are those who do not have any position on which they enter in futures and options market. They only have a particular view on the market, stock, commodity etc. In short, speculators put their money at risk in the hope of earning profit from an anticipated price change. They consider various factors such as demand, supply, market position, open interests, economic fundamentals and other data to take their positions.

Spin Off: When a company decides that a subsidiary needs to stand on its own, it might do a spin-off, distributing shares of the new entity to existing shareholders, or selling the new business to its managers or even its employees.

Spoofing: Placing a limit order at a better price than the current market price for purchase or sale of thinly traded scrips and then endeavouring to cancel the initial limit order with a view to induce buy or sell.

Spot Delivery Contract: A contract which provides for: (a) actual delivery of securities and the payment of a price therefore either on the same day as the date of the contract or on the next day. The actual period taken for the despatch of the securities or the remittance of money therefore through the post is excluded from the computation of the period aforesaid if the parties to the contract do not reside in the same town or locality, (b) transfer of the securities by the depository from the account of a beneficial owner to the account of another beneficial owner when such securities are dealt with by a depository.

Spot Price: The price at which an instrument/asset trades in the spot market.

Spread: It is the difference between the buying and selling prices of a currency.

Square Position: When sales and purchases of a currency are equal, it is known as a square position. It is also called *square book, flat book* or *matched book.*

Stag: An applicant, for a new issue of shares, who hopes to sell the shares on allotment at a profit once trading commences in the secondary market. It can also mean a speculator who buys and sells stocks rapidly for fast profits.

Stagflation: The combination of sluggish economic growth, high unemployment and high inflation.

Stagnation: Period of low volume and inactive trading on the securities market.

Stakeholder: Any individual or group who has an interest in a company, viz. shareholders, workers, consumers, suppliers, the local community and so on.

Stamp Duty: A tax on documents dealing with such matters as transfer of property, shares, debentures, and insurance policies. If unstamped, these documents become invalid. Stamp duty (or transfer tax) is generally collected through the sale of revenue stamps which must be affixed or imprinted on the document in question. Stamp duties are often under the jurisdiction of state and local governments.

Standard Price: The standard price of a security is generally worked out as a weighted average price of all recorded transactions for that security adjusted to the nearest rupee.

Statutory Liquidity Ratio (SLR): See Reserve Bank of India, *184*.

Stock Exchange: Any body of individuals, whether incorporated or not, constituted for the purpose of assisting, regulating or controlling the business of buying, selling or dealing in securities.

Stock Index Future: A futures contract whose price varies in line with the movements of a stock market index.

Stock Lending: The lending of a security by the registered owner, to an authorized third party, for a fixed or open period of time, for an agreed consideration secured by collateral. The demand to borrow securities comes mainly from market makers to cover short positions or take arbitrage opportunities.

Stock Market: A stock (or share) market deals mainly in corporate securities. The securities are chiefly in the form of equity shares and debentures. The purpose of these securities is to raise long-term funds for companies engaged in production. The function of the stock market is two-fold: (a) to arrange for the raising of new capital (primary market function), and (b) to provide liquidity to existing securities (secondary market function).

The new capital is raised by the issue of shares and debentures. The corporate enterprises raising new capital may be new companies or existing companies planning expansion of their operations. Sometimes, existing private firms go public, i.e. become public limited companies.

The stock market helps the floatation of new issues by providing a variety of services like underwriting, distribution, and listing of the issue. Underwriting means guaranteeing the purchase of a fixed amount of new issues by the underwriter. The new issues of capital may be a public issue or a rights issue or both in certain proportions. It may be in the form of equity shares or debentures. Debentures, in turn, may be fully convertible, partly convertible, or non-convertible into shares. A public issue implies that the general public is invited to subscribe to the new issue. A rights issue is restricted for subscription by existing shareholders.

Stock market provides facilities for secondary market, i.e. transaction in existing securities. People desirous of converting their cash into securities can go to the stock exchange and buy securities with the help of brokers there. Similarly, securities can be converted into cash by selling them in the market. Transactions in the secondary market reflect the investment climate in the economy.

A well-developed stock market helps to access external capital which allows financially constrained domestic firms to expand. It is argued that countries with developed stock markets tend to grow faster.

Limitations of Stock Market: It is argued that stock market expansion is not a necessary indication of a country's financial development and stock market development may not help in achieving quicker industrialisation and faster long-term economic growth because of following reasons:

1. Due to inherent volatility and arbitrariness of the stock market, the resulting pricing process is a poor guide to efficient investment allocation.
2. In the wake of unfavourable economic shocks, the interactions between the stock and currency markets may exacerbate macroeconomic instability and reduce long-term economic growth.
3. Stock market development is likely to undermine the financial inclusion role of existing banking systems in developing countries like India.

Stock Option: The right to purchase shares of common stock in accordance with an agreement, upon payment of a specified amount. It is a kind of compensation scheme under which executives are granted options to purchase common stock over an extended option period at a stated price.

Stock Splits: A distribution of company's own capital stock to existing stockholders with the purpose of reducing the market price of the stock, which would hopefully increase the demand for the shares.

Stop Loss Order: An order to sell a security when it declines to a specified price.

Straddle: A combination strategy in which the same position is taken in the same number of puts as calls.

Straight through Processing (STP): The processing of a trade, whose data is compliant with internal and external requirements, through systems from post-execution through settlement without manual intervention. Simply put, it means seamless integration of trades from initiation to settlement without manual intervention.

Stress Testing: Stress testing is used to evaluate a bank's potential vulnerability to certain unlikely but plausible events or movements in financial variables. The vulnerability is usually measured with reference to the bank's profitability and/or capital adequacy.

Strike Price: The stated price per unit for which the underlying index may be purchased (in case of a call) or sold (in the case of a put) by the option holder upon exercise of the option contract.

Sub-account: Sub-account includes foreign corporates or foreign individuals and those institutions, established or incorporated outside India and those funds, or portfolios, established outside India, whether incorporated or not, on whose behalf investments are proposed to be made in India by a foreign institutional investor (FII).

Sub-broker: Any person—not being a member of a stock exchange—who acts on behalf of a stock broker as an agent or otherwise for assisting the investors in buying, selling or dealing in securities through such stock brokers.

Subordinated Debt: It refers to the status of the debt. In the event of the bankruptcy or liquidation of the debtor, subordinated debt has only a secondary claim on repayments, after other debts have been repaid.

Subscribed Capital: The amount of equity and preference capital subscribed to by the shareholders either fully or partly paid up with calls in arrears.

Supervisory Review Process (SRP): SRP envisages the establishment of suitable risk management systems in banks and their review by the supervisory authority. The objective of the SRP is to ensure that the banks have adequate capital to support all the risks in their business as also to encourage them to develop and use better risk management techniques for monitoring and managing their risks.

Swap Buyback: The sale of an interest rate swap by one counterparty to the other, effectively ending the swap.

Swap Reversal: An interest rate swap designed to end counterparty's role in another interest rate swap, accomplished by counterbalancing the original swap in maturity, reference rate, and notional amount.

Swap Transactions: These are transactions in which a currency is bought and sold simultaneously but delivery dates for the purchase and sale are different. Net exchange position remains the same even if there is a change in the spot rate of the currencies.

Swaps: Swaps take many forms but often entail the exchange of one type of asset or payment for another. Some of the more common forms are the following: cross-border, currency, debt-for-charity, debt-for-commodity, debt-for-debt, debt-for-development, debt-for-equity, debt-for-export, debt-for-local-currency, debt-for-nature, discount, dual currency, interest rate, inward, premium, reverse, and vanilla. Minor variation in names is common.

- **Currency swaps** convert principal from the lender's currency into the debtor's currency and receiving interest payments in the debtor's currency.
- **Debt swaps** entail replacing the foreign liabilities of a debtor country with ownership or rights of value.
- **Debt-for-equity swap** replaces foreign liabilities with a stake in the debtor country's national enterprises.
- **Debt-for-export swap** replaces foreign liabilities with an arrangement to receive proceeds from the overseas sale of the debtor country's products or commodities.
- **Debt-for-debt swap** replaces an existing foreign liability with a new commitment from the debtor country.
- **Interest rate swaps** involve agreements on the means for exchanging future cash flows.
- **Single currency interest rate swaps** concern exchanging future cash flow in the same currency and offer a means for modifying the impact of future changes in interest rates on a company's profitability.
- **Cross currency interest rate swaps** concern exchanging future cash flows between one currency and another, traded either on a fixed or floating rate, and offer a means for limiting the risk of converting financial interests between currencies.

The swap—made to protect the principal from future changes in foreign exchange rates—involves a forward exchange contract to recover the currency involved. Swaps also involve arrangements whereby different sellers of similar commodities swap and deliver them to each other's customer if such action saves transportation costs. See also Credit Derivatives, and Financial Derivatives.

Swaption: Options on interest rate swaps. The buyer of a swaption has the right to enter into an interest rate swap agreement by some specified date in the future. The swaption agreement will specify whether the buyer of the swaption will be a fixed-rate receiver or a fixed-rate payer. The writer of the swaption becomes the counterparty to the swap if the buyer exercises.

Sweat Equity: A sweat equity share is an equity share issued by the company to employees or directors at a discount or for consideration other than cash for providing know-how or making available rights in the nature of intellectual property rights or value additions.

Synchronized or Pre-arranged Trading: Trading on the electronic screen in such a way that trades are put simultaneously in the system of the stock exchange with prior understanding with counterparty by synchronizing the logging in or of trades so that desired quantity matches at desired price.

Systemic Risk: Risk that affects an entire financial market or system, and not just specific participants. It is not possible to avoid systemic risk through diversification.

Tt

Takeover Panel: An acquirer who proposes to acquire shares through a mode which is not specifically covered under takeover regulations may seek exemption from the applicability of the provisions of the offer process by making an application. SEBI has constituted a panel consisting of independent persons to examine such applications. It is called the Takeover Panel.

Taligating: When a broker purchases or sells a security for his client and then immediately does the same transaction in his own account. This is not illegal like front running, but is still considered to be unethical because the broker is usually placing a trade for his own account based on what the client knows (like inside information).

Target Company: A target company is a listed company i.e. whose shares are listed on any stock exchange and whose shares or voting rights are acquired/being acquired or whose control is taken over/being taken over by an acquirer.

Tata Strategic Management Group (TSMG): It is one of the leading management consulting firms in South Asia.

Technical Position: Condition of the market created by various internal factors and opposed to external forces.

Tender Offer: Tender offer means an offer by a company to buy back its specified securities through a letter of offer from the holders of the specified securities of the company.

Thin Markets: It is characterized by relatively few transactions per unit of time and where price fluctuations are high relative to the volume of trade.

Tier I Capital: A term used to refer to one of the components of regulatory capital. It consists mainly of share capital and disclosed reserves (minus goodwill, if any). Tier I items are deemed to be of the highest quality because they are fully available to cover losses Hence it is also termed as core capital.

Tier II Capital: It refers to one of the components of regulatory capital. Also known as supplementary capital, it consists of certain reserves and certain types of subordinated debt. Tier II items qualify as regulatory capital to the extent that they can be used to absorb losses arising from a bank's activities. Loss absorption capacity of Tier II capital is lower than that of Tier I capital.

Time of Recording: The time of recording for transactions and, hence, for holdings is governed by the principle of accrual accounting. For financial claims and liabilities, changes of ownership are considered to have taken place at the time that the parties to the transactions record them in their books or accounts. If no precise date can be fixed, the reporter may use the date on which the creditor received payment or the date on which some other financial claim was satisfied. For direct investment income data, dividends should be recorded as the date they are payable and income on debt as it is accrued.

Time Priority: Time priority means if two orders having the same price are entered, the order which entered the trading system first gets the highest priority.

Tombstone: An advertisement placed in financial newspaper or magazine to announce the completion of a syndicated loan or a new issue of securities. It is called a tombstone because it consists of little more than a list of names and dates. The names are those of borrower (who pays for tombstone) and of the financial institutions which participated in the deal. They are ordered in strict seniority, the size of the typeface indicating their importance in the deal. Within the same rank, participants are listed strictly alphabetically. The more the tombstones there are, the less dead is the market.

Total Return Swap (TRS): See Credit Derivatives, *49*.

Trade Netting: A legally enforceable consolidation and offsetting of individual trades into net amounts of securities and money due between trading partners or among members of a clearing system. A netting of trades which is not legally enforceable is position netting.

Trading Member: A member of the derivatives exchange or derivatives segment of a stock exchange who settles the trade in the clearing corporation or clearing house through a clearing member.

Transaction Statement: It is a statement given periodically by a depository participant (DP) which gives details of current balances and various transactions made through the depository account. If so desired, DP may provide the transaction statement at intervals shorter than the stipulated ones, probably at a cost.

Transactor Principle: There are two principles that may serve as the basis for geographic allocation of financial flows: the debtor/creditor principle and the transactor principle. Under the transactor principle, transactions resulting from changes in the claims and liabilities are allocated to the country of residence of the non-resident party to the transaction (the transactor), even if this is not the country of residence of the direct investment enterprise or direct investor. See also Debtor/Creditor Principle.

Transfer Agent: An agent designated by the company to carry out the function of transfer of shares.

Transfer Form: A form which has to accompany the share certificate for effecting a valid transfer of ownership from the seller to the buyer.

Transferee: It means the buyer of the securities in whose favour the securities are bought to be registered.

Transferor: It means the seller of the securities.

Transparency in Transactions: The National Stock Exchange (NSE) introduced screen-based trading at its inception in 1992 which was followed by other stock exchanges. Screen-based trading makes online, electronic, anonymous and order-driven transactions possible. It is a transparent system which provides equal access to all investors, irrespective of their geographical locations.

The move to an electronic trading system has resulted in transparency in trades, better price discovery and lower transaction costs. The efficiency of the market has improved through faster execution of trades. The operational efficiency of the stock market has also been strengthened through improvements in the clearing and settlement practices and the risk management process. Almost the entire delivery of securities now takes place in dematerialised form. Over the past few years or so, there has been no instance of postponement or clubbing of settlements at two main stock exchanges (BSE and NSE) despite defaults by brokers. The cases of bad deliveries are close to nil. Insider trading has been made a criminal offence. Non-transparent products like *badla* have been banned.

The setting up of trade/settlement guarantee funds in most of the exchanges has considerably reduced settlement risks for investors. Corporate governance practices and disclosure norms have led to transparency in information flows, which in turn have improved the price discovery process.

In order to bring greater transparency to the debt market, and to move away from bilateral negotiation towards anonymous order-matching, trading in government bonds began on stock exchanges on January 16, 2003. This has involved exploiting the identical process flow used for trading in equities. Trade takes place by anonymous order matching for all orders across the country, risk management is done by the clearing corporation, and settlement takes place at the depository. Under this system, government bonds appear in the depository statement of an investor alongside corporate equities and bonds. This system has several strengths.

1. Anonymous trading avoids the supervisory and regulatory difficulties of the telephone market, where counterparties are aware of identities and can engage in trades at off-market prices.
2. This market design offers symmetric market access from locations all over India and over the internet, as opposed to the telephone market, which favours entities in south Bombay.
3. It exploits information technology to guarantees that orders are matched against the best price available in the country. This is in contrast with the telephone market, where traders can search for counterparties, but are not sure of having found the best counter party.
4. It is fully transparent in that orders and trades are visible in real time. This is in contrast with the telephone market, where orders are not visible, and the transparency of trades is limited and delayed.
5. It exploits the information technology of the depositories of the equity market (NSDL and CDSL), which have the full range of functionality required for investors such as a wide network of IT-enabled depository participants, internet access, strong computer security, access to data about the beneficial owner down to the end-investor.

Issuers also have the option of raising resources through fixed price mechanism or the book building process. Book building was introduced to improve the transparency in pricing of the scrips and determine proper market price for shares.

Treasury Bill: A short-term bearer discount security issued by governments as a means of financing their cash requirements. Treasury bills play an important role in the local money market because most banks are required to hold them as part of their reserve requirements. Open market operations of a central bank, in the process of implementing monetary policy, are usually conducted in the treasury bill market.

Trust Deed: Detailed legal document which sets out in precise legal terms the rules under which a trust works, its aim, the fees and charges that are created, plus the responsibilities of the manager and the trustee. As per SEBI Debenture Trustee Rules, trust deed is a deed executed by the body corporate in favour of the trustees named therein for the benefit of the debenture holders.

Trust Promoter: Person or company responsible for attracting investors into a unit trust or mutual fund.

Trustee: Legal custodian who looks after all the monies invested in a unit trust or mutual fund.

Uu

Underlying: The designated financial instrument which must be delivered in completion of an option or futures contract.

Underwriter: A financial organization that handles sales of new securities which a company or municipality wishes to sell in order to raise money. Typically, the underwriter will guarantee subscription to securities (say an issue of equity from the company at a stated price), and is under an obligation to purchase securities up to the amount he has underwritten, should the public not subscribe for the issue.

Underwriting: An agreement with or without conditions to subscribe to the securities of a body corporate when the existing shareholders of such body corporate or the public do not subscribe to the securities offered to them.

Undistributed Profits Tax: It is imposed on companies which allow their retained profits to accumulate beyond the reasonable needs of business. Companies may prefer to hold profits rather than pay dividends so that their shareholders could postpone personal income taxes that would have to be paid if the dividends were paid out. The undistributed profits tax attempts to checkmate this practice on the part of companies.

Unit Holders: Investors in unit trusts/mutual funds.

Unit of Trading: See Marketable Lot, *127*.

Unit Trust of India (UTI): Set up in 1964, it reflected the efforts of the Government of India to popularise unit trusts and mutual funds in the country to encourage indirect holding of securities by the public. The UTI was established to mobilise the savings of the small investors who constitute the bulk of India's population.

Government has extended various types of concessions including tax benefits to UTI and its unit holders. The UTI with a large investor base, has been running various schemes including the flagship, US-64, various assured returns schemes, and other NAV-based schemes. Recently, important decisions have been taken to tide over the financial problems faced by the UTI. On October 28, 2002, an ordinance was promulgated which repealed the UTI Act, and created two entities, UTI-1 and UTI-2. UTI-2 is an unencumbered mutual fund, with only NAV-based schemes. UTI-1 has US-64 and the assured returns schemes. On 15 January 2003, the handover of UTI-2 to a new set of owners (State Bank of India, Bank of Baroda, Punjab National Bank and Life Insurance Corporation of India) took place.

Unmatched Transactions: A check is carried out to find out whether the purchases and sales as reported by the members match. Those transactions which do not match are called unmatched transactions.

Unsystematic Risk: It is the risk that is unique to a company, such as a strike, unfavourable court judgement in a litigation, or a natural catastrophe. Also called company-specific risk.

Upstairs Market: A network of trading desks for the major brokerage firms and institutional investors that communicate with each other by means of electronic display systems and telephones to facilitate block trades.

UTI: See Unit Trust of India, *219*.

Vv

Valuation of Stocks: Using market price as the basis for valuation. However, it is recognised that, in practice, book values from the balance sheets of direct investment enterprises (or investors) are often used to determine the value of the stock of direct investment.

Value Added Tax (VAT): Value added tax is levied on the sellers of goods and services based on value added by their respective units. The base of VAT is determined by value added at a particular stage of production or distribution. Meaning of VAT becomes clearer when it is juxtaposed against conventional turnover tax (excise duty, sales tax) which falls on the total value of the product at each stage of production chain and is called a *cascade* type tax. VAT, a fiscal innovation of early 1960s, has claimed world-wide attention as more and more countries are adopting it in varying degrees to reform their system of commodity taxation.

Value at Risk (VaR): VaR is a single number (currency amount) which estimates the maximum expected loss of a portfolio over a given time horizon (the holding period) and at a given confidence level. VaR is defined as an estimate of potential loss in a position or asset/liability or portfolio of assets/liabilities over a given holding period at a given level of certainty. The following are the three main methodologies used to calculate VaR:

1. **Parametric Estimates:** VaR is estimated by using parameters such as volatility and correlation. The technique is accurate for traditional assets and linear derivatives, but less accurate for non- linear derivatives.
2. **Monte Carlo Simulation:** It estimates VaR by simulating random scenarios and revaluing positions in the portfolio. It is appropriate for all types of instruments, linear and non-linear.
3. **Historical Simulation:** It estimates VaR by reliving history;

takes actual historical rates and revalues positions for each change in the market.

Value Investing: The investment style of attempting to buy under-priced stocks that have the potential to perform well and appreciate in terms of price.

Vanilla Issue: A straight fixed rate issue which has terms and conditions usually accepted as being conventional to a particular securities market.

Vanishing Companies: Companies which have not complied with specific provisions of the listing agreement and regulations of the stock exchanges, and are not physically traceable at the registered address mentioned in the offer document.

Variation or Mark-to-market Margin: All daily losses must be met by depositing of further collateral (known as variation margin), which is required by the close of business, the following day. Any profits on the contract are credited to the client's variation margin account.

VAT: See Value Added Tax, *221*.

Venture Capital: Professional moneys co-invested with the entrepreneur, usually to fund an early stage, more risky venture. Offsetting the high risk is the promise of higher return that the investor takes.

Venture Capital Fund: A fund established in the form of a trust or a company including a body corporate and registered under the SEBI venture capital fund regulations. It has a dedicated pool of capital, raised in a manner specified in the regulations, for investments in venture capital undertaking in accordance with the regulations.

Vertical Spread: Buying and selling puts or calls of the same expiration month but with different strike prices.

Volume of Trading: The total number of shares which change hands in a particular company's securities. This information is useful in explaining and interpreting fluctuation in share prices.

Voluntary Delisting: Delisting of securities of a body corporate voluntarily by a promoter or an acquirer or any other person other than the stock exchange.

Voluntary Reporting Requirements: Situations where there is no legal obligation for reporters to provide the requested information.

Voting Rights: The entitlement of a shareholder to exercise vote in the general body meeting of a company.

Voting Stocks: These are shares that give voting rights to the holder. These can either be *listed voting stocks* (i.e. shares that are listed on an official stock exchange), or *unlisted voting stock* (i.e. shares that are not listed on a official stock exchange.

Ww

Warrant: An options contract often sold with another security. For instance, corporate bonds may be sold with warrants to buy common stock of that corporation. Warrants are generally detachable.

Wash Sales: A wash sale involves a person, either directly or indirectly, being both the buyer and seller of securities in the same transaction, so that there is no actual change in ownership of the securities. The manipulator will undertake frequent trades hoping to attract other investors who note the increased turnover in the security. The manipulator aims to gain financially through creating a small price differential between the buy and sell rates of the security in question.

Window Dressing: A manoeuvre often engaged in by companies, banks, mutual funds etc. at the end of the accounting period in order to impress stock holders who will be receiving the report showing that funds are better managed and invested than what might have been drawn up.

Wolf: Speculator who makes a kill in the market.

Worst Case Scenario Loss: It is calculated by valuing the portfolio under several scenarios of changes in the underlying prices and volatility. The maximum loss in any situation is referred to as the worst scenario loss.

Writer: A person who issues an option. The individual who at the end of the day has to buy or sell the asset, on which the option is written, should the person who holds the option wish to exercise his rights.

Written Down Value: It is the value of a depreciable asset determined by deducting from the actual cost the depreciation allowances granted by income tax authorities in previous tax years. Actual cost – Depreciation = Written down value.

Xx, Yy, Zz

X-efficiency: The concept of X-efficiency, attributed to Harvey Leibenstein, is an important issue in economic development. It is basically concerned about why people do not work as hard or as effectively as they could. In other words, X-efficiency deals with how human inputs affect economic development. X-efficiency is generally contrasted with allocative (or static) efficiency.

Yankee Bond: A bond offering in the US domestic market by a non-US entity registered with the Securities and Exchange Commission (SEC) (q.v.).

Yield-to-maturity (YTM): YTM is the yield promised to the bondholder on the assumption that the bond will be held to maturity and coupon payments will be reinvested at the YTM. It is a measure of the return of the bond.

Yuppie Scam: The name given to Wall Street insider trading scandal after a host of smart young lawyers, bankers and arbitrageurs were found to be in the dealing ring.

Zero Bracket Income: It is that amount of taxable income which is taxed at a rate of zero percent. Under the Indian Income Tax Act, 1961, the first slice of income of ₹ 2 lakh of a general category individual is taxed at zero percent (financial year 2013-14). It is also called basic exemption.

Zero Coupon Bond: A bond that pays no interest while the investor holds it. It is sold originally at a substantial discount from its eventual maturity value, paying the investor its full face value when it comes due.

Zero Coupon Yield Curve: A yield curve of zero coupon bonds. It is a market practice to derive this curve theoretically from the par yield curve. Frequently used to derive discount factors. Also known as spot yield curve.

Zero Rated Goods: Under Value Added Tax (q.v.), there are sometimes zero-rated goods like food, newspapers and medical prescriptions. For such goods, no VAT is charged on output but VAT suffered on inputs is reclaimable. Hence, zero-rated goods escape entirely from VAT. On the other hand, there are services like postage, education, and health which are exempt from VAT. No VAT is charged on these services but no VAT can be reclaimed on inputs. Hence, exempt goods do not suffer any tax on the value added at the final stage.

Zero Tax Company: Income tax laws usually provide for a host of deductions and incentives to promote socio-economic objectives of state policy. It is likely that a profit-making company may arrange its affairs in such a way that the cumulative effect of all deductions is to reduce its income declared in the tax return to zero. To deal with such situations, some countries have introduced Minimum Alternative Tax (q.v.).